The INFJ
User Guide

The
INFJ
User Guide

The complete guide to
the INFJ personality

Sarah Kuhn

Printed in the United States of America.

Design by Sarah Kuhn

Names: Kuhn, Sarah, author.
Description: First edition. | Boston, MA.
Identifiers: ISBN 978-1-7349954-0-4 (ebook) | ISBN 978-1-7349954-1-1
(hardcover)

Disclaimer: I am not a lawyer, and this should be considered legal advice. You
should seek appropriate counsel for your situation. And please note, this post
is directed towards readers in the United States. If you're conducting business
or purchases outside of the United States, I highly recommend you find and
understand your obligations regarding disclosures in your residing country.

First Edition: April 2020

This book is dedicated to every INFJ. May you always be aware of the magic within you and your personality and what a gift you are to the world.

Contents

Introduction

I've been searching for self-love for a long time. My life has felt like one big audition with the judges being my family, friends, co-workers, and even bosses. I'd give them my all and exceed their expectations, only to find out I was never good enough to make the cut. This feeling has always eluded me, shredding my mental state to pieces, trying to understand if something was wrong with me. I'd ask myself; why am I not enough? How do I fix myself? It wasn't until last year, in 2019, that the answers to an old test opened my eyes to the true meaning of self-love. It helped me recognize everything it had taught me about myself over the years were all detours down the wrong road to get me on the right path to self-love. Although I didn't always enjoy the detours, it's been the most fulfilling journey. I'm learning how to love myself, march to the rhythm of my beat and help others love themselves on a deeper level.

In my quest for an understanding of self, being accepted by others and having a positive outlook of my life, I stumbled upon an MBTI test I had taken back in college. And there, in plain black and white, I found all the answers I'd been looking for. Bingo! The test results were bleeding green, answering every question I'd secretly been asking myself ever since I was a little girl.

When I was young, I was painfully shy, hiding behind my mom and my older sister every chance I could to avoid talking to anyone. Words rarely made it out of my mouth, that when I spoke, people would gawk at me in disbelief. The piercing of their eyes was so uncomfortable, I vowed to never utter another word again. Most days I succeeded.

Growing up in what seemed like a glasshouse, had some benefits as I was forever the good girl who won my parents' favor by my obedience. I always did what I was told to, lending a helping hand to my sisters and brother, working until I completed all the chores. My older sister and I were the best of friends, as long as I did what she wanted me to do. When I refused, she'd transform into the nastiest enemy, ready to fight to the death. It was a constant battle between whether I wanted to go along with her or avoid her altogether. My little sister was the outcast we hated. She was too young to take part in whatever we had going on. My brother came along when I was 10 years old and he was the living doll I loved to take care of.

I begged to know why I was so different from most of my peers growing up. Building the courage to talk to the other kids in my class only made it clearer how different I was. Their eyes lit up as the topics of the latest fashion and trends, who's dating who and what's popular in music echoed throughout the classrooms. I would pass up conversations about any of that and secretly long for the more important things to me.

I got goosebumps discussing what books to read, writing assignments vs talking, and doing word puzzles. I longed to engage in something that was challenging and fun, such as spending my free time doing extra credit to make sure I was a straight-A student. Being the teacher's pet was a piece of cake to me, even though my classmates didn't enjoy my praises from all the teachers. Truth is, on the inside I was sick to my stomach being put in the spotlight and often suffered the consequences of being so, by always finding myself eating lunch alone. No one saw a young girl willing to do anything to help because that's how much I cared. All they saw was a girl who thought she was smarter than others whom the teachers loved. Deep down inside, living in the shadow of that lie hurt my feelings every day.

I pleaded to know why I always felt disconnected and easily misunderstood by others. In college, it was the same story, just a different day. I was there to learn, not party or make friends. I had accepted that most people didn't like or understand me, so I gave up trying. I sat in the front of class and soaked up the course materials, enjoying every minute of my higher education. I loved it so much I spent 10 years in college. One half of me didn't know what I wanted to do with my degree, and the other half loved being in that setting and learning every day. I studied business, marketing, criminal justice and several kinds of engineering.

I spent years in a counselor's office and on Google trying to figure out what was wrong with me. When I discovered my personality type, so much of my life made sense. I finally felt like it was ok to be me. I finally had proof that all those people who had told me I needed to talk more or open up more were wrong! I felt so relieved!! I soaked up every bit of information I could find about being INFJ. I wanted to know it all and make sense of my whole life.

That's what led me to write this book just for you. We're connected in ways we've yet to discover as INFJs. I know you understand what it feels like to be criticized and ridiculed for being different. No one's cared to go the extra mile to understand you, they'd rather commit to misunderstanding you. You know all too well what it's like to move mountains for others but hide under a rock when it's time to fight for yourself.

Even though there's still much to learn about INFJs, this book is for those who've recently discovered you're an INFJ. It's designed for INFJs who're tired of feeling alone and ready to meet other fellow INFJs worldwide. The ones who've committed to being open to grow and deepen their self-love for themselves. I can't wait to share with you everything I've learned throughout my journey of healing and self-love. Find out what I gave myself more of before it finally clicked. I discovered just how much of an impact our personality type is to the community, making up 1% of the world population.

We're here for a reason, and I want to share with you the exact tools you need to join me on this journey. It all starts with knowing exactly what an INFJ is.

The INFJ
User Guide

1

What does INFJ Mean?

What is an INFJ? What does it even mean? The term INFJ comes from the Myers Briggs Type Indicator (MBTI) personality test. Their theory, based on the work of Carl Jung, says that everyone in the world falls into one of 16 personality types. It makes those personality types up of 4 categories.

- Introvert/extrovert
- Intuition/sensing
- Feeling/thinking
- Judging/perceiving

INFJ is an initialism that means introvert, intuition, feeling and judging. This means we are introverted - we recharge by spending time alone, intuitive - we just know things, feeling - we decide based on our gut feeling and judging - how we decide and organize our lives.

The rarest of them all

The INFJ personality type, sometimes referred to as the Advocate, is the rarest of all personality types, making up less than 1% of the population of the world.[1] That sounds like a scary statistic, like there aren't very many of us, so we will never meet another one and no one will ever understand us!

Hold on for a second, though. Let's put it into perspective. As of April 2020, the estimated population of the world is over 7.7B people.[2] That's many people! Even 1% of 7.7B, which is 77,000,000, is a lot. Some studies say that up to 3% of the world population could be INFJ, so that's 231,000,000!

That means the total number of INFJs in the world is somewhere between 77M and 231M. Those numbers give us a lot of hope! As INFJs, the biggest things we are looking for are understanding and connection. I'm certain we can find that within our own personality type and most of all, I'm very certain we are not alone at all!

Being an INFJ makes us unique in several ways. We like people but need alone time. We use both the thinking and feeling sides of our brains. We like to dream about things, but we also like to put those dreams into action. We spend a lot of time avoiding people, but we do truly want to help them. We are full of contradictions.

We need alone time

As introverts, we recharge by being alone. This means we need to spend time alone. Not only is it something we enjoy, but it's necessary for our health. Being around people drains our energy. The more time we spend around others, we deplete our energy. The only way to recharge that energy is to be alone. So we spend large amounts of our time alone. We really enjoy this time and look forward to it every day.

Thinking and feeling

We use both the thinking and feeling sides of our brain. We can use logic and reasoning, but we can also go with our gut feeling, which we usually rely on. Because we can use both sides of our brain, we can see situations and problems from all kinds of angles. We spend a lot of time thinking through these things to come up with the best solution for everyone in every situation.

Overly thinking of others

We have an extroverted feeling, so we think about other people's feelings before we think about our own. We are constantly thinking about the surrounding people to make sure they are comfortable and they have what they need. We like to make people happy and keep things peaceful around us.

Soft-spoken with strong opinions

As introverts, we are laid back and quiet. We like peace. We enjoy harmony among our friends and family. Our friends even say we have a soft and comforting voice.

However, with morals and values, things we really believe in, we have very strong opinions and we aren't afraid to share them. When we really believe in something, we will fight to the death for it.

Dreamers and doers

We have very strong and active imaginations. The inside of our head is often our favorite place to be. We like to imagine what could happen, how things could turn out. We have high hopes for our lives, reaching for the stars in a lot of ways.

Not only are we good at dreaming big dreams, but we are also good at taking actions to make those dreams come true. We have the will and the determination to do whatever it takes to accomplish our goals.

Finding our purpose

INFJs have this inborn need to find their purpose. It's been there ever since we can remember. High school and college are the most challenging times of our lives because we just don't know what we want to do with our lives. We want to fulfill this purpose, but we do not understand what it is. For some of us, it feels like a lifelong journey to find this thing. We look under every rock and in every crevice, searching for the meaning of our lives.

Some of us are lucky to find it early in our lives. Others don't find it until much later. Most INFJs will tell you that their purpose finds them. When they find it, they just know. Their intuition leads them to the thing they are supposed to do, and they enjoy knowing what it is and doing it every day.

A lot of INFJs tell me their purpose has changed throughout their lives. It's not just one thing, but there can be many things.

If you haven't found it yet, keep looking. You will.

Helping others

Because we are so focused on and in tune with how other people feel, we often want to help them in any way we can. A lot of INFJs find themselves in service-related careers, such as counseling or social work, because they want to help people every single day. Some of us take a less direct approach and instead try to help people by sharing our knowledge through writing or podcasting. Whatever approach you take, you are probably thinking about how you can help someone in your work and your life. It's always close to the front of our minds.

So different

Because we only make up 1-3% of the population, a lot of INFJs grow up feeling like we are out of place. We notice how different we are from most other people. We have listened to people tell us we are wrong for years. They tell us we're wrong for being too quiet and not having enough friends. They criticize us for wanting to read rather than playing outside. They question why we'd rather wander through a museum alone than go to a bar to dance with people.

Because we pay so much attention and are so concerned with how other people feel, we collect these things that people say to us and take them to heart. Eventually, we believe them. We think of ourselves as being wrong. We wonder if we are broken or messed up.

- Why did I have to be born like this?

- Why can't I just be like everyone else?

- It's such a difficult burden to carry around with you, especially early in our lives.

As we get older, it feels a little better because we normalize it. We already know we're different, so we are. We eat lunch in our car rather than socialize with our coworkers. We avoid going out because we don't like the noise and the people. We stick to our one or two friends because they let us be who we are. We stick to the lives we've carefully curated because they feel safe and easy. We don't go too far outside of the lines because we don't want to open ourselves up to that hurt and rejection that we've felt so many times before.

I spent years in this space, feeling the weight of my differences like a 100 pound rock on my back that nearly crushed me every day. I accepted the fact that I was not like anyone else and that no one would ever understand me. I toyed with the idea in my head from time to time, but never really had a solution or an answer.

When I was in college, I studied Engineering for a while. I took lots of classes about reasoning and questioning what you thought you knew. I took statistics, which I hated, but I learned a valuable lesson from that class: you can make statistics say anything you want them to. You can manipulate them to fit the result you want. So now, every time I read a statistic, I question it because I know how they work.

I started thinking about my personality in the same way.

- Who told me I was wrong for being different?
  Too many people to count, really.

OK, so lots of people.

- Why do they think I'm wrong?
  Because I'm not like them. Because they don't understand why I'm not like them, so they assume I'm wrong.

This is the most important question of all...

- Why do I believe what they are telling me?
  Well, because it's my mom telling me these things. It's my dad, my grandma, my sister, my best friend, my teacher, my boss, my spouse. Surely they know, right?

But do they really know? Maybe they are all extroverts. Maybe they are different introverts. Maybe they have sensing personalities or thinking personalities. Maybe someone told them they were wrong for their whole lives too, and they are just telling you what they believe to be true.

Here's what I know to be true

After much thought and analyzing these things, I've concluded that there is a lot of miscommunication and misunderstanding that has been passed down for generations. There's a lot of accepted beliefs that are not true.

You are not broken or messed up. I want to say that again, so you really hear it. You are not broken or messed up. You are different from most other people. That doesn't mean you are wrong.

You've always been able to see the world differently. You process thoughts and feelings differently. You decide differently. You organize things differently. Different does not equal wrong. Different means that you are not the same as someone else. And whoever decided that was wrong was confused.

It made you this way on purpose

You are not wrong at all. You are not an extra or a reject. However, you believe you came into being, whether it's a Higher Power or something else, however you were made it was on purpose and for a good reason. There's a reason you are looking for your purpose because it designed you with a need to fulfill that purpose.

You are perfect just the way you are. You need not change anything about your core personality. Sure, there may be improvements you want to make. We are always looking for ways to improve and do things better. But your core personality is perfect. You need not change how you recharge or how you decide. And you can't do that anyway, no matter how hard you try!

Your personality is unique and amazing! It's a wonderful thing to explore. I challenge you to look at it through new eyes, to set down all the things you've been told about yourself. I want you to ask the questions:

- Who told me I was wrong for being different?
- Why do they think I'm wrong?
- Why do I believe what they're telling me?

I want you to think about the possibility that you aren't broken or messed up and consider what your life would look like if you understand yourself better. Think about what it would be like if others took the time to understand you.

What if, instead of hate and disgust, you looked at your differences with patience and grace?

What if you really understood what it means to be introverted? Would you just accept someone telling you it's wrong to be alone to recharge? Or would you challenge their opinion and educate them instead?

What if by understanding yourself better you could help make the world a nicer and kinder place to live?

I hope you find that understanding in the pages of this book. My hope and desire is that it's a tool for you to get to know yourself and for you to accept who you are and embrace it. This information has been life changing in that way for me, and I hope it does the same for you.

What happens when you finally understand

When you finally understand your personality, so much changes. You feel like a different person. The world in a whole new light.

Sierra Mafield explained her experience in an interview I did with her on my podcast, The Quiet Ones.[3] "I know myself so much better. This is a classic INFJ thing; you think you're so complicated and you don't even understand yourself. You're like, 'Why am I so different from everyone else?'

"When I read through everything... it's definitely resonated with me. That just makes me feel so much better because sometimes there are some things where I'm just like this weird, weird person and then I'm like, Oh, but wait. It's an INFJ thing. It totally works out!

"Overall, it makes me feel like I make more sense in the world and I'm not like this weird alien that was just plopped down from another planet. That's a simple thing, but it's just that sense of inclusion in something else with someone else. Even if we are a rare breed, it makes me feel so much better."

Laura Charelle had a similar experience, which she also shared in my podcast.[4] "Once I read the profile, I was like this makes so much sense why I do what I do.

"Growing up, I learned real quick that it was more socially acceptable to be extroverted. So I overcompensated in a lot of situations trying to be extroverted, but then didn't understand why I would feel so exhausted when I would get home or I would be away from people. It helped emotionally, to have that release of knowing it's OK to be this way. It's OK to go to a party for an hour or two and then leave and know that you've had your fill of socializing."

Discovering your personality and learning the characteristics of it will completely change your view of yourself and the world around you. We spend our entire lives looking for that kind of understanding and acceptance. It starts right here and right now.

2

Introvert

What does it mean to be an introvert?

Dictionary.com defines being an introvert as:

1. A shy person.
2. A person characterized by concern primarily with his or her own thoughts and feelings (opposed to extrovert).[5]

I hate to tell them they have it all wrong. In fact, every dictionary I checked had a similar definition. Perhaps this is where so much confusion starts around this word. Many people confuse being shy with being introverted. But I assure you they are not the same.

Where your Energy Comes From

Being an introvert is not the same as being shy. Being introverted means that you gain energy by being alone. A lot of us refer to this as recharging. We spend time alone to recharge our internal batteries and feel we have the right amount of energy needed to carry on in our lives. Some of us need a lot of alone time as being around people drains our energy rather quickly. But it's not just people, it's the quality of conversations and connections we have with people that drains us. But we'll speak more on that later.

The opposite of introvert is extrovert. A lot of times it's confused with being outgoing or talkative or liking people, but again, this is a misapplication of these terms. Being extroverted means that you gain energy from being around people. You feel recharged when you spend time with your friends and your family. You also enjoy meeting new people and being in places where many people are. All of this gives you more energy.

There's a third option here as well that's called ambivert. This is someone close to being right in the middle. They are equally drained and recharge by being around people. Sometimes they feel and act as an extrovert and want to spend time around large groups of people. Other times they feel and act as an introvert and need alone time by themselves. Many people fall into this category.

The difference between shy and introverted

There is a huge difference between being shy and being introverted. Being shy means that you are afraid to talk or shun attention. Being introverted means you recharge by being alone. Does that sound the same to you? Me either.

The same goes with the difference between being outgoing and extroverted. Outgoing means you like to talk to people, you're friendly and sociable. Being extroverted means you recharge by being around people. Though this one sounds more similar, I assure you they are different things.

The fact is, you can be a shy extrovert and an outgoing introvert. You can also be a shy introvert and an outgoing extrovert.

I'll give you an example from my life. I'm a tried-and-true introvert. When I take the MBTI test, it comes up close to 90% introverted. But when I go places, like the grocery store or to work, I like to chit chat with the people I see, make them feel comfortable and encourage them in any way I can, even if it's just a simple "I hope you're having a good day" or laughing about something simple. In that area of my life, I'm friendly and sociable, the definition of outgoing. But I recharge by spending time alone. That's my happy place.

The inside of my head is my favorite place to be

My favorite thing about being introverted is my imagination. I love the inside of my head! It's my favorite place to be. I have a constant story going on there that is my ideal life. It changes from time to time, but it's always there. It's like the best movie I've ever seen or the best book I've ever written. It's a vivid and intense dream that makes me want to stay for a while, any time I can.

It's also a great place to test out new ideas or theories that come to me. We like to think our ideas through before we present them to someone else. We may spend weeks or months thinking something through before we've concluded that we're ready and willing to share. It's a process that takes time for us to look at all the angles and connect all the dots.

The introvert in everyday life

When you're introverted, you like to spend time alone, often large amounts of time alone. You are quieter and more reflective, because you like to think about things before you say them out loud. Your hobbies are typically calm and nourishing things, enjoy reading, studying new ideas and figuring out puzzles.

You enjoy things that are calm and quiet. The busy streets and loud clubs that many people enjoy make you easily overwhelmed. You learned from a young age that you can only take in so much noise and commotion before you must retreat and recharge again. It drains your energy much more quickly than something more relaxed and less involved. You're more likely to spend your Saturday night in bed watching a documentary about serial killers or the environment.

You only have a few friends that you've selected carefully. You value your time and energy, and you make sure that they do the same. You would much rather have a deep conversation about the meaning of life with one good friend than spend a night out on the town with a group of people you barely know. It's quality over quantity every time.

You order food from an app on your phone because talking to the people in the store can overwhelm you. You'd much rather just grab your coffee and go. You avoid those restaurants that ask you 100 questions before you can get your burrito, because the pressure of saying all the right words in the right order and as soon as they ask you is just too much for a Tuesday lunch. You'd rather pick what you want from a screen and have it delivered to the office. You're even ok with the extra cost just to avoid all the other people out at lunch, in traffic and in the restaurant.

Your work is also calmer. You prefer spending your days doing something alone or in small groups of people. You are more likely to be in a career where most of your work is done alone and you have the freedom to take breaks when you need to. You appreciate a boss who understands your lack of enthusiasm for large meetings and group projects. You also have multiple tricks up your sleeve to avoid staff engagement activities and any kind of mandatory office fun, like company outings and office birthday celebrations. Your co-workers know you will only show up for a short time to get a piece of cake and then go back to your desk. They've accepted this about you a long time ago and respect you for it.

Dating is a challenge for you. You hate the apps that lack connection and deep conversation and you hate going to new places and meeting new people. Because of your lack of enthusiasm for the process, you stayed single longer than your friends. You had other things that interested you.

When you do finally meet the right person, they mean a lot to you. You connect with them on a deep level and you get to know them more than you have ever known anyone else. You share things with them you have never shared with anyone out loud. If they are introverted too, they completely understand your need for alone time and you even enjoy your alone time together. If they are extroverted, while it's fun that they take you to new places and push you to get out more, perhaps about your need for alone time. But you come to an agreement, and they respect you setting boundaries.

When you have kids, you forget what alone time feels like. The constant noise and demand on your attention is a whole new kind of draining that you didn't know existed. The only thing that makes it better is when your little monster grabs your face and says, "I love you!" Your heart melts as you wince at the sloppy, chocolaty kiss that was just planted on your chin. You wonder if you have enough cash for a babysitter so you can take a bath by yourself tonight and recharge.

It's OK to be quiet

There is a common idea that being introverted is wrong or it means something within you is broken, it's something that needs to be corrected. When I was young, I was constantly being told to speak up more or take part more in class discussions. When I got older and started applying for jobs, I noticed a lot of them said, "must be extroverted and enjoy being around people." It's like they had this idea that introverts don't like to talk and wouldn't enjoy being around people.

This idea that being introverted is an issue that needs to be overcome is a big misconception. There is nothing wrong with being quiet. There is nothing wrong with wanting and needing to spend time alone. There is nothing wrong with ordering food from an app and not wanting to attend a staff engagement activity. It doesn't mean you're broke. It makes you different from the rest of the crowd. But different is not the same as wrong.

Being introverted isn't something that needs to be fixed, it's not a problem you have to change. It's a part of your personality just the same as making decisions based on your gut feeling such as being organized vs messy. This is how you gain energy. You may even try to change it. But it's not something you can change. You can act like you've changed it and live as if you have, but at some point, you'll crash and need to recharge again.

It's OK to differ from most people. It's even OK for them to not understand. You can consider their thoughts and ideas without taking them to heart. Accepting that you're introverted and that you need alone time to recharge will help you understand yourself and give yourself more grace when the demands on your time are too high. It will also help you set standards for how the people in your life will treat you. You need time and space to think and breathe and be, and that's perfectly OK.

3

Intuition

The second letter in the Myers Briggs Type Indicator personality type tells us how we process information. Do we take everything at face value (Sensing) or do we read between the lines and see the bigger meaning behind what we say (Intuition)? For INFJs, we fall into the intuition category.

But what does being intuitive mean? Dictionary.com defines it like this:

1. Direct perception of truth, fact, etc., independent of any reasoning process; immediate apprehension.
2. A fact, truth, etc., perceived in this way.
3. A keen and quick insight.
4. The quality or ability of having such direct perception or quick insight.[6]

Through this definition we see that there are 4 different intuitions. Some personality types will experience one or more of these, though very few types use all of them together. Some personality types have intuition as a dominant function, meaning they use it frequently and for some it's buried in the background and they barely know it exists. What makes INFJs different is that we use all 4 types of intuition all the time.

The words "immediate apprehension" in the definition of intuition caught my eye. The best way that I can describe intuition is that I just know. I just know what I know about something or someone, even if I have no proof or concrete evidence. I get a feeling that's overwhelming and impossible to ignore.

I've tried to ignore this feeling many times. A lot of times I'll get a feeling of intuition about something that's completely out of the blue or realm of possibility. Or it will be something that no one else sees or understands. So, I try to ignore it and carry on. But then, more times than not, I'm proven to be right. That feeling really was something. I've learned to not ignore it, but to lean into it. The more I listen to it and the more I trust it, the stronger it gets.

I like the way Francis P Cholle described it in Psychology Today:

"Intuition is a process that gives us the ability to know something directly without analytic reasoning, bridging the gap between the conscious and non conscious parts of our mind, and also between instinct and reason."[7]

What he's saying is that there isn't always a logical, step-by-step process for how we get to what we know. It's more of a combination of things we see, experiences that we've had, ideas that we've considered and so on, and it all comes to us in a flash that's hard to explain. Let's look deeper.

What is intuition?

As INFJs, our intuition leads our thought process. It's the strongest function we have, making up a large part of our personality. Intuition in the ability to know things that most other people don't.

Because this is mostly a subconscious process and because most people don't experience intuition, it's often seen as something magical or spiritual. INFJs are thought of as prophets or fortune-tellers.

The process of Introverted Intuition is not magic at all, actually it's a simple process. INFJs observe what's going on around us in great detail. We notice everything. Through this observation, we collect all kinds of information and organize it in our minds. We are constantly looking for patterns and connections to make it all make sense. We then take these patterns and apply them to future scenarios to "predict the future."

Most people who have intuition experience this process on a subconscious level, meaning that it really isn't noticeable. They know that they just know things, but they don't know how they know. An underdeveloped or young INFJ will feel the same way.

However, as we get older and become more aware of the process, we see what is going on in real-time. We notice that we are noticing things and making connections between them. It's not always at the front of our minds, so we do still experience the phenomenon of just knowing something, but we also understand how it works and trust the process more.

Intuition is a collection of all of our communication gathering abilities. As INFJs, we are great at noticing a lot of things quickly. When we're talking to people, we don't just think about what they say. We take in a lot more than that. When we observe a man in a store that we don't know we can tell a lot about him just from observing him. We notice what he's wearing, those sneakers that look brand new with the logo that reminds you of something expensive you saw in the mall the other day. We notice the black pants bunched up at the top of the sneakers, like they are too long. We also see the wrinkles in them and their slight discoloration that tells us they've been worn for a while. We take in the white t-shirt and the comfortable hoodie that looks like it's soft.

We look at those striking collar bones just beneath the sharp, masculine lines of his jaw. Then there's the weak smile that shows in his mouth, but doesn't reach his eyes. There are crows feet there, but they aren't showing with this expression. His brown eyes don't sparkle with this look, but you know they do at other times. His dark hair, that points straight up, lightens just above his ears, betraying his age.

He holds his hands, one inside the other, and immediately looks away when he sees you look at him. You can see the anxiety in his tense shoulders and his quick movements.

It may have taken you a moment to read the description, but as INFJs, we take in all of this information in an instant. Automatically, with no conscious thought or action, we are looking at these things and making connections. Within a split second, without even knowing where it came from, we just KNOW. Our intuition is telling us something about this guy. Sometimes it's a marked thought like "He's in trouble. Can't you see it?" Other times it's a more subtle feeling nudging you to pay more attention to him, see what else you can see and feel.

Some people would refer to this knowing as being psychic or clairvoyant, but that's not the conclusion I'm trying to draw here. I don't for a minute think we are psychic, though I'm certain some INFJs are psychic. Being psychic is not the same thing as being intuitive, though. The things that our intuition tells us, the things we just know, are a collection of information, conscious and subconscious. Though it seems very mysterious and perhaps majestic, it's not supernatural.

We see things in patterns. We see the whole picture at once, the main story in a flash. That's the just knowing part. Then we set to work figuring out all the details and the facts of the situation. That comes afterward. Sometimes these pieces fall into place in a flash, but often they take a lot more time and effort to figure out and connect.

We make these connections by thinking about the possibilities. We experiment with different ideas and scenarios until we come to what we think the most logical solution is. Then we examine the evidence again to see if it fits. If it does, we go back to examining to make sure we didn't make it fit.

Have you ever seen an INFJ so deep in thought they did not understand what was going on around them? This could be why. It's a whole process, but it's also a fun process for us. We love to have a puzzle to solve and a question to answer. It's our favorite pastime.

Let's go back to the description of the guy. As you notice that guy standing in the store, in a split second you just know he's in trouble. You get a feeling that he's not ok. If you know this guy or have to spend some time around him, you analyze that feeling a little deeper. You can see that his shoulders are tense and the way he's holding his hands seems like he's anxious. You know that because you do the same things when you're anxious.

A lot of times you're left here, wondering if that feeling is correct and why you felt it in that moment. Sometimes it's very clear and other times it's not clear at all, especially when it's a stranger and you will probably never see them again.

In my experience, our intuition will jump out at us right at the right time. I started a new job one time and the very first time I met my boss I had a feeling he was not a good person. It was perplexing to me that everyone in the office liked him and called him a nice guy, even though they all admitted he was horrible at his job and did almost nothing well. Time and time again my intuition was proved right while I was at that job.

Another time I met someone and knew right away that I would like him. The feeling that I got when meeting him was a lot softer and more gentle. He was friendly and kind. No matter what I told him, he listened with an open mind and was very helpful and encouraging. We became good friends and are still good friends to this day.

It's also very effective when you are talking to someone you know. My niece called me one time and was telling me about this terrible problem she had. She told me a long story about how she got into this problem and was asking how she should fix it. I was trying to put the pieces together as she was talking, actively leaning on my intuition. In a flash I knew her story was not true, not because of anything that she said, but I just knew. And I was right. She was dumbfounded how I just knew what really happened. I couldn't explain it, other than I just know.

It's not just people

Our intuition guides us to know situations, not just people. We look for patterns in events and everyday life activities. We can see things happening before they happen through the same process we use on people. We collect information about past and current events and predict the patterns for future events. This makes us amazing planners for life events and for work events. We are wonderful project managers and can keep things on track effectively because we can see what's coming better than most people.

How to use & improve it

There are many ways you can use your intuition. The first thing you have to do is pay attention. It's not something you can get if you don't have it, but if you're INFJ you have it, even if it doesn't seem that way. It's that little voice that's telling you something every once in a while. Sometimes it's like a soft, gentle whisper and other times it's like a freight train that smacks you in the face! You can't miss it! But if you have ignored it for a long time, then it may not work very well. You just have to be still and listen for the whispers.

When you hear one of those whispers, pay attention. You don't have to announce it to everyone or do anything even. You just have to notice and observe. Make a note of the whisper and what it's telling you. Then think about how it would affect you if it were true. What would you do? How is that different from what you were already planning to do? Is there a way that you can prove or disprove it? If not, then just sit back and see what happens. The more that you listen to these whispers and find them to be true, the more you will hear them and the louder they will be. It will become second nature to you.

It's not something that you can make happen though, unfortunately. It's something that comes and goes as it pleases. But, like I said, the more you pay attention to it, the more often you will feel it.

Let's talk about it

One thing I've learned is that people who don't have intuition don't understand it. When you try to tell them about it, they don't get it. They want some kind of solid proof of what you're trying to tell them. A gut feeling will not convince them of anything.

These are the people who will undermine your confidence every time you share something with them. They only believe things they can see and touch, so they will try to convince you that what you feel isn't real. In my experience, it's best to let them be. Don't convince them you are right. In fact, don't even share your feelings with them. They don't understand and you won't be able to change their mind. You'll just end up getting hurt and losing confidence in yourself and your intuition by trying.

Intuition in everyday life

You pay attention to lots of things all the time. You notice things that most people don't see. You often get feelings about things that you can't explain, but you know them to be true.

You have a feeling when you get into your car about your commute to work. You take a different way to work than normal, which takes a little longer, but you feel better about it. When you get to work, someone tells you that there was a bad car accident on the road you normally take. They are surprised and relieved to see you at work because they thought it could have been you in the accident. You search for news of the accident Online when you get to your desk and see it was a red Toyota Corolla in the accident. You drive a red Toyota Corolla. It freaks you out all day long by the similarities and try not to let your mind wander to the "what if's."

You notice a friend at work hasn't been in the break area as much as normal. When you see him everything seems OK, but you just know something is wrong. You spend some time wondering if your feeling is right, but second guess yourself so you say nothing. Your friendship continues to wane and you keep going back to that feeling of something being off. Eventually you ask him about it, and he tells you it has nothing to do with you. He's going through a hard time at home and is even struggling to make it to work. You wish you would have listened to the feeling sooner and reached out to him when you first felt it.

A blessing and a curse

I feel like intuition is both a blessing and a curse. It's nice to know things sometimes, especially when you can help someone because of that knowledge. If you can take away their pain or make their life even easier, it's a huge blessing. But the curse comes when you know something and you can't do anything about it, but you still know it. It also comes when you just know something, when you have a bad feeling, but you can't figure out what the feeling is or why. It's not always clear, and sometimes it never becomes clear.

A lot of the blessing and curse comes with how you use it. Are you making the most of it and listening to yourself? Are you trusting your feelings and watching to see what happens? There is a lot more good that comes from it than bad. It's all about how you use it.

Feeling

The third letter in the Myers Briggs Type Indicator personality type tells you how you decide. Are you focused on logic and reason (Thinking) or are you more focused on people and going with your gut feeling (Feeling)?

For INFJs this third letter is feeling, but don't confuse feeling with being emotional, because those two terms do not mean the same thing. Let me explain.

My experience

I was so upset when I found out I was an INFJ. I was mistyped for years as an INTJ and I loved feeling like I was tough and analytical. I didn't want to be emotional or to be seen as emotional. I have always worked very hard to keep my emotions to myself. They are very, very personal to me and I don't share them with hardly anyone.

In 2017, I had told my niece, 13 at the time, about the MBTI test. She took it and became obsessed with her type, INTP. We were having a conversation one day about personality types, and I was trying to explain to her why her grandma was upset with her. She had hurt her grandma's feelings, and I was trying my best to explain why, based on personality functions. She's very analytical, so it made sense to her to think about the situation in these terms.

My niece looked at me in the middle of my explanation and said, "I don't think you have a thinking personality. I think your personality is feeling. You're always talking about feelings and concerned with people's feelings. I'm not like that at all. I'm always focused on logic and reason."

I was shocked and horrified. I didn't want to have a feeling personality type at all! I thought it was mean that she would say something like that. I really thought having a feeling personality type meant that I had to be outwardly emotional. I also thought it meant I had to be very dramatic with crying and yelling and throwing angry fits.

But when the initial shock wore off, I analyzed what she meant a little more. Can you have a feeling personality type and not be emotional? How does that work?

The difference between feelings and emotions

There is a huge difference between feelings and emotions. Bryn Farnsworth, Ph.D., in his article How to Measure Emotions and Feelings (And the Difference Between Them) explains,

"Imagine this: You sprint through the airport, on the run, to catch your flight. While you try to make your way through the crowd of people waiting in line at the security check, you spot an old friend you haven't seen in ages. Before you can say anything, you tear up overwhelmed with excitement (and forget about the rush) while you give your friend a firm hug.

"Emotions are lower level responses occurring in the subcortical regions of the brain… [and] are associated with bodily reactions that are activated through neurotransmitters and hormones released by the brain, feelings are the conscious experience of emotional reactions.

"Feelings are sparked by emotions and shaped by personal experiences, beliefs, memories, and thoughts linked to that emotion. Strictly a feeling is the side product of your brain perceiving an emotion and assigning a certain meaning to it"[8]

Basically, that means that emotions are triggered by a chemical and/or hormonal change in your brain, while feelings, triggered by a different part of your brain, are deeper and more meaningful. Feelings are more a part of your personality, while emotions are a passing reaction to a low-level trigger, like happiness and anger.

What does having a feeling personality type mean

Having a feeling personality type does not mean that you are outwardly emotional all the time or that you are that way. INFJs are known for being rather stoic, keeping their thoughts and feelings to themselves most of the time. We place so much meaning on our feelings; we don't want to share them with just anyone. You have to be special to us in order for us to feel comfortable enough to share our feelings with you. It doesn't happen often.

Just because we don't show our feelings to everyone doesn't mean that we don't have feelings. Just because we don't show them doesn't mean they aren't there. In fact, we have deep and powerful feelings. We spend a lot of time thinking through ideas and analyzing different concepts. We scrutinize every idea and concept from every angle we can imagine, and then we start over and do it all again. It's important for us to consider an idea from every angle we can come up with before we share it with anyone else.

We also spend a lot of time thinking about our morals and values. We have a "life code" that we live by and want to make sure that what we are doing is right, not only for us but for all the people in our lives.

Extroverted feeling

Part of our personality is called Extroverted Feeling. That means we are more concerned with what other people are thinking and feeling than with what we are thinking and feeling. We spend a lot of time thinking about other people. We test how our loved ones are affected by the things we do and say. We consider what they want before we think about what we want. We notice when they are upset and want to fix it quickly, no matter what caused it.

This applies to everyone around us, anyone we come in contact with. We notice their mood, posture, and the feeling that we get when we are around them (remember that intuition?). If we aren't careful, we can soak up these feelings and become overwhelmed easily. We take these things on as our own. Because we are so focused on everyone else, we may not even notice that we are overwhelmed at first. We just know that we are tired and need to rest.

How you handle being overwhelmed

Self-awareness is the key to not becoming overwhelmed by other people's emotions. It takes an active awareness on your part of what is happening to you when you are around other people. I'll give you an example that has happened to me many times.

I'm standing in line at the grocery store, already anxious because I have to be in the store around many people and I don't want to be there. So I'm on high alert with my own emotions. Then I notice someone in front of me getting really angry about something. Sometimes I can tell what's making them mad, and other times I can just see that they're angry.

As soon as I noticed they were angry, I felt tense and uncomfortable. I don't want to be there at all. I get even more anxious than I was before and start looking for a faster way out. When I can escape the situation, pay for my things and leave the store, I feel a weight lift, but I also still feel heavy. It's like I'm worried about this poor angry man in the store and I do not understand why.

In the past I would carry that weight with me, not knowing where it came from or how to get rid of it. And the weights would collect. The angry man in the grocery store, the driver behind me who was not happy that I had to make a left turn, the lady on the phone who was annoyed that I forgot her name twice, my boss who's always overworked and upset, my friend who sounded annoyed that I called her, my mom who never has enough money, etc. I was anxious and overwhelmed and drained all the time.

It took me years to realize that I was carrying these emotions with me. I cared for each one of these people and the impression or feeling that I gave to them, regardless of whether it came from me.

I learned that just because I experience those emotions at the moment doesn't mean that I need to take them with me. I can notice the angry man and not feel his anger. I can leave it there in the store. His anger doesn't belong to me. It belongs to him. I don't have to take it with me when I leave him. This goes for every person on the list, regardless of whether you know them and whether you live with them. You don't have to take on their feelings and emotions. They don't belong to you. You can set them down and go about your day without them.

How do you set down everyone else's feelings?

Every time I feel overwhelmed, I find a quiet place to sit and think for a while. I ask myself a few questions:

- What am I thinking about?
- What's weighing on my mind, maybe even in the background?

- Where did I get it from?
- Does it belong to me?

That last question is the most important. Does it belong to me? If the answer is no, then I put it down. There is nothing that I can do or change by worrying about it, even if it came from my mom or my spouse or my child. Thinking and worrying about it won't make it better. And if it doesn't belong to you, then it's best to put it down. You need not carry it around with you anymore. It's OK to set it aside.

Sift through everything that you've taken on. The more you do this, the easier it will be to do it at the moment, when you are feeling the emotions of the angry man or the annoyed phone lady. You won't have to take on their emotions anymore, but feel them at the moment and then set them down right then. It's such an empowering feeling to know that you have a choice!

How you express your feelings

INFJs often have a difficult time expressing our feelings and emotions. We are always thinking about how everyone around us will feel or react and always wanting to keep the peace in every situation. It's easy for us to fall into the people-pleaser role and hide our feelings and emotions. We opt to make everyone else happy and reason that this makes us happy.

Eventually, always giving in to everyone else will create a complicated problem for us. Every single day, with every decision, we teach people how to treat us. When we always give in to what they want, they assume that they will always get what they want every time they interact with us. When we do speak up, things can get dicey, because the people we have surrounded ourselves with aren't used to it and they don't know how to react.

I'll give you an example. When I was growing up, I was shy. I rarely said anything to anyone. Even when I got my first job, I rarely said anything to my co-workers. When I said something, everyone would look at me like I had 2 heads. Sometimes they would say things like, "You talk?" I took that as a personal insult and made sure not to speak up anymore.

By doing that, backing down and not calling them out for being so rude, I taught them it was OK for them to treat me like that. And they did, for as long as I worked there.

Later in my life, just this past year actually, I was at work, talking to 3 of my male co-workers. One of them interrupted me mid-sentence to make a negative comment about me wearing sandals in the wintertime in Boston. "Who wears sandals in the wintertime? Don't your feet get cold?" Everyone stopped to look at my feet. It mortified me that he had called me out like that and drawn so much attention to me. I looked him right in the eye and said, "Are you the fashion police? What does it matter to you what shoes I wear? I never even notice your shoes." I said it in a half-joking, half don't mess with me tone. He got the idea that it was not OK to talk about my shoes like that.

We teach people how we treat us. We tell them what's OK, and what's not. While we are much more prone to bottling up our feelings inside and going along with what everyone else wants, it's important for us to speak up and ask for what we want and need. I know it feels selfish. It's not. It's important that we place as much value on ourselves and our own wants and needs as we do on everyone else's.

How you decide

Another place that our feeling personality type is important is how we decide. People with thinking personality types decide based on facts and logic. Those of us with feeling personality types decide based on a gut feeling or what we desire, rather than what is reasonable. We think about what feels right for us.

Now, this gets a bit complicated for INFJs. We use both the thinking and the feeling functions in our brains, so you may notice a bit of a war going on when you have an important decision to make. It's almost like there are 2 people in your head yelling at you. One is all about logic and reason, and the other is all about what you feel you want or what seems right in your heart. It can be a huge mess trying to figure out what to do. We usually go with our gut, or what we feel is right.

It's hard for us to explain this process to others and also hard to explain why we made certain decisions. People ask me all the time why I moved from Kansas, where I grew up, to Boston. I have a few logical reasons that I've thought out. There are more job opportunities in a bigger city and more people, so more chances of me meeting a future spouse and friends. But the cost of living is significantly higher. So it doesn't seem very logical.

But it wasn't a decision based on logic either. It felt like the right thing for me to do. I knew in my heart and my gut that I should move. I saw all kinds of signs that I should move, and I jumped at the chance to go. That's a classic INFJ decision. It's more about intuition and feeling than anything else.

Feeling in everyday life

You feel things deeply, even if they don't belong to you. You notice not only your own feelings and emotions, but the feelings and emotions of everyone around you. You are constantly analyzing situations to come up with the ideal solution for everyone involved. You like to keep the peace and make everyone else happy. You also decide based on how you feel about something rather than what is logical.

Your friend wants to throw you a birthday party, but you hate parties with a passion. You accept her offer anyway because you don't want to hurt her feelings and you truly value her friendship and her desire to make you happy. You hate all the small talk that goes with parties, but you act happy to make your friends happy, especially the one that organized everything. You open presents in front of everyone, being careful to make sure your face has the appropriate amount of joy and surprise with every gift. Inside you're dying because the gifts are not only useless and provide no value to you at all, it actually hurts you that your friends don't know you any better. You go home exhausted from hours of pretending to be happy and being around people and wonder how long you have to keep their gifts before you can throw them out.

You are trying to decide what to have for dinner. The logical side of your brain is saying stay home and eat a nice healthy salad. The feeling side is saying you should get a sandwich from your favorite place. You reason that the place is a 45 minute drive and you hate traffic and you really don't want to go that far after work. You know that it's a lot of effort for dinner and you could spend your time doing something else, like the laundry that's been piling up. You get in the car and head to get the sandwich because you feel like it's a good idea and you really want it.

The truth of the matter

Having a feeling personality type is not good or bad. It's just how you process things and how you decide. It can feel like a lot, especially if you keep everything on the inside and let nothing out. It can feel like a curse if you buy into the idea that you have to please everyone else and get nothing you want or need. It doesn't have to be that way, though. You can make it what you want it to be. You teach people how to treat you. You have taught them for years and you can teach them something different now.

Deciding based on how you feel is not a bad thing either. It's the way you process your thoughts. When you add in your intuition, it makes perfect sense.

5

Judging

The fourth letter in the Myers Briggs Type Indicator personality type tells you how you show the decisions you make to everyone outside of you. Are you spontaneous and easy-going (Perceiving) or are you more planned and organized (Judging)?

For INFJs this third letter is judging, but don't confuse judging with being judgmental towards others, because those two terms do not mean the same thing. Having a judging personality type explains how you show the decisions you make to the world. Being judgmental means that you are making negative assumptions about people and events. They are not related at all.

How you use your feeling function to decide

As INFJs, our feeling function, explained in chapter 4, helps us a lot with this last function: judging. It influences how we decide. When we decide, we use our extroverted feeling to think about how our decisions affect everyone else. We like to have things planned and organized so that everyone is on the same page and knows what's going on. We want everyone to feel comfortable in any situation we're involved in.

One reason we excel in school and at work is because we are great at deadlines. We enjoy getting things done on time and getting the credit for that achievement. To accomplish these goals, we relish things like calendar apps, checklists, planners, highlighters, and file folders. We love anything that makes us feel like we have our lives organized and together.

Not only do we consider what other people need in our decisions, we consider what they think. We know that we are being monitored in certain areas of our lives, like in college and at work, and we like to keep our appearance up to our high standards.

High expectations and standards

INFJs are known to have high standards and expectations for themselves and for others. We are constantly noticing things we want to change and looking for ways to improve ourselves. It's a natural part of our ability to notice things that others may not. We love searching for answers to problems and making things better, faster, easier, and more efficient.

Our high standards often lead us to big achievements in our lives. We're the students with high grade point averages and the workers with impressive resumes. We can learn things quickly and easily and are always looking for something new to tackle.

We dream big dreams. We want things in our lives that many people would dismiss as impossible or unattainable. We see these things as possibilities though and get to work figuring out how to make them happen. It's another puzzle for us to figure out. We thrive on these types of puzzles, and the desire to improve and achieve drives us forward. Sometimes we get so focused on the goal that we lose sight of everything else. Finding a life balance in these situations is crucial for our health and wellness.

The nightmare of looking for your purpose

In the last chapter, we spoke about how INFJs need to find our purpose. We are born with a desire to do something meaningful with our lives, but we do not understand what it is. This journey quickly becomes a nightmare for most of us because we like to have things settled and decided. We need a goal to achieve, and that needs a solid plan. When you don't have a goal, you can't have a plan. Instead of feeling decided and secure in your efforts, you end up feeling like you're lost in the dark and you'll never find your way out.

An INFJ that doesn't have a goal, or a plan is a scary thing! It's easy for us to lose all hope and fall into depression because we don't know what to do with ourselves. We like to be in control of our lives and when that feeling is missing we spiral down a dark hole of despair.

INFJs need control

Most people think of INFJs as being laid back and easygoing, and we are to a point. The thing is, we like to have some control over our lives. We like to know what's going on, to know what will happen and to plan for everything we can think of. To do these things, we need to have some kind of control over our lives.

We like things that are predictable and repeatable. We look for patterns in everything we see, people, situations and events. We like to connect the dots and use this information for future planning. We combine our trusty intuition and our introvert powers of observation to decide about our lives and the surrounding people.

These things make us wonderful planners. We can consider and plan for lots of contingencies and make things work in a lot of different situations. We're scrappy when we need to be and will figure out whatever it takes to get things done. But to get things done, we have to be in control. We have to have the power and ability to take charge and decide.

This does not mean that we're the scary cartoon character that's trying to take over the world. Not at all. We are more the laid back type that would rather someone else takes charge and tell us what to do. We are great at following directions and getting things accomplished.

The problem arises when we lose faith in the leader or when there is no leader. We are not ones to blindly follow someone who we don't believe in. If they are making decisions that do not benefit the most people or that violate our values and morals, we will quickly lose all respect for them, regardless of their title or position. There is no going back.

When there is no leader, it's hard for us to just go with the flow of the crowd, especially if everyone is lost and confused. We see the inefficiency of the situation and our desire to help overcomes our desire to stay quiet.

In both situations, we will stand up and take charge of the situation because we feel like it's the best way to help, even though we hate being in charge and telling people what to do. We see what will help and benefit the most people. We see where things can improve and what needs to be done to meet the deadline. We aren't afraid to take charge when we need to.

Control in our own lives

INFJs need control in our own lives. We are at our best when we can make our own decisions and plan our own lives. It's comforting for us to know what's coming and what we need to do to accomplish our goals.

In unhealthy INFJs, this need for control can turn into an obstacle pretty quickly. When we are in a situation where we feel like we have no control, we might look for that feeling of control in other places. We turn our focus to something we can control, like how we look. We'll make sure that our appearance is "just so" by spending a lot of money we don't have on nice clothes or exercising way too much. Some of us may even develop an eating disorder born more out of a need to control something in our lives than the actual food itself or the way we look. It's important to reach out for help if you find yourself in any of these situations. I've been there. I know how hard it is, but it's necessary for your health to get out of that situation and on to something better.

What it means on the inside

It's important to us to have things together on the outside. We like organization and to achieve our goals. What goes on inside can be much different, though.

The inside of the INFJ brain is a complete mess most of the time. We are so organized on the outside because we can't keep track of things unless they are written and scheduled, with little reminder notifications that are seriously lifesavers. The inside feels like rabid squirrels bouncing off the walls most of the time. There are so many thoughts and ideas happening all at once. There is so much information being taken in and processed. There is so much past information to go through. No wonder it could take 6 months for us to figure out how we feel about something!

On the inside, we are much more flexible than we appear on the outside. We consider new ideas before we are ready to share them with the world. We have to process what they mean to us and consider all the options, get our arguments and defense in order before we are challenged by anything outside of us.

We spend a great deal of time considering what we are doing and how it affects everyone around us. We think things through thoroughly before we announce an outside move. Every life choice that we make has been well planned and thought out. This is one reason we take so much offense to people's judgments and criticisms of what we do. They do not understand the amount of effort we have put into our plans. We've thought of everything we can imagine and planned for every contingency. Sometimes it's easy to forget that they don't see this or have any way to know it.

Judging in everyday life

You like to have things under control. You enjoy having decisions made, making a plan and sticking to the schedule. You want to know what will happen before it happens and have a backup plan. You like to consider everyone involved in every situation and want to make sure your plan includes everyone and accounts for their comfort and convenience.

You know what a disaster planning dinner on the fly can be. You always seem to get home and have only half of the ingredients that you need to fix what you wanted to. Or you are half-way through cooking dinner when your spouse comes home with pizza. You get hurt when this happens because you don't feel that your efforts are recognized and appreciated and your family is always more interested in pizza than the healthy dinner you are trying to serve them. To mitigate this problem, you create a monthly schedule for dinner. You plan a whole month's worth of dinner, being careful to consider what each family member likes to eat and to include take out nights and going out to dinner. You announce the plan to your family and meet their looks of annoyance and protest with a firm desire to fix what you see as a big problem. It's what's best for everyone and you won't back down from it.

You work for a company that has a "there are no leaders here" philosophy. They are all about teamwork. The problem is with no one in charge nobody knows what to do so nothing gets done. The owners complain that nothing gets done, but still stick to their flawed philosophy. You are involved in planning a big event for your customers, and you want to make sure the customers have a great time. So, while you look for a new job because you don't agree with the company philosophy, you take charge of the event planning. You organize what needs to be done and assign tasks to certain people. You schedule planning meetings and set deadlines for tasks to be accomplished. Because of your efforts, everything with the event is accomplished on time and under budget. The event runs smoothly, and the customers are happy.

You are 25 years old and feeling lost because you haven't found your purpose in life yet. You keep thinking if you look under enough rocks, if you study hard enough in school or if you read enough books, it will come to you, but it hasn't yet, and it discourages you. People tell you it will come to you, but you think maybe it got lost somewhere, or maybe you did. You felt like all hope is lost because you do not understand what to do. It weighs on you every second of the day. You finally realize that the problem is you feel lost. You need to not feel lost. To fix this feeling, you make a plan. You start with what you like to do and what you want to do, which is writing about boy bands (because who doesn't love boy bands?!?), even though you do not understand how you'll make money doing this. You create a detailed plan to start a blog and start writing about something you love. You dive into research about blogging and immediately feel a sense of relief that you have a plan and you are making progress on it. You don't know if this is the right thing to do or if it will work, but you like the feeling of doing something. As time goes by and you keep writing and learning, you realize that your focus has changed to starting a business. While it's easy to feel you wasted your time blogging about boy bands, you realize that you learned so much in that process and you never would have figured out how much you like business if you hadn't started that blog. You don't feel like that time was wasted. Instead, you value the time you spent learning and share your experience in your new business.

The decisions we make

There is a lot that goes into every decision we make. It's not just about what we feel like we want at the moment. Sometimes we spend months or even years planning the best course of action. We think and plan and rethink and plan again until we are sure of the course. Putting things down on paper is a great source of clarity for us because we can organize our thoughts and plans better that way.

No matter how much we think and plan, the best course of action for us is to just take some action. Clarity in all of our decisions comes from deciding. So often we just get stuck in the planning stage and take no action. Because of this, we slide down the dark hole of despair. The only cure for that is action. Do something. Take action. Decide, even if it's the wrong decision. The wrong decision will probably lead you to the right decision, eventually.

6

Functions

So far in this book, we have spoken only of the Meyers-Briggs personality type preferences (Introvert, Intuitive, Feeling, Judging). Preferences help us understand what our personality type is and give us a general understanding of who we are and how we operate. But they only give us half of the story. We also have to look at Functions.

According to Carl Jung, four of the eight preferences, Sensing, Intuition, Thinking, and Feeling, can be introverted or extroverted. When they are introverted, they are something that we feel but don't show to the world. They happen on the inside. When they are extroverted, they are something that we show to the world. They happen on the outside.

The 8 Functions

1. Extroverted Thinking (Te)
2. Extroverted Feeling (Fe)
3. Extroverted Intuition (Ne)

4. Extroverted Sensing (Se)
5. Introverted Thinking (Ti)
6. Introverted Feeling (Fi)
7. Introverted Intuition (Ni)
8. Introverted Sensing (Si)

Though there are eight functions total, you only have four of them in your personality. Those four make up your functional stack, which we'll get into later. For now, let's look at what the functions mean.

Extroverted Thinking (Te) - looks to make any operation or procedure more logical and standardized. They look for the most efficient and rational way to do things and apply it to everything.

Introverted Thinking (Ti) - looks to make their own personal decisions logical and standardized. They are more focused on the individual rather than the whole experience.

Extroverted Feeling (Fe) - looks at all the feelings of those around them. They want to have peace and harmony among everyone.

Introverted Feeling (Fi) - looks at their own feelings and focuses on their own values and inner harmony.

Extroverted Intuition (Ne) - looks for new ideas and possibilities to explore outside of themselves. Ne types love learning new and deep ideas to keep them thinking about what could be.

Introverted Intuition (Ni) - explores ideas and possibilities that come from inside.

Extroverted Sensing (Se) - looks for exciting experiences outside of themselves, things that appeal to the senses (taste, sounds, sights, experiences).

Introverted Sensing (Si) - relies on their own experience that they know is tried and true. They don't like new experiences, but would rather go with what they know works.

Functional Stack

Dominant Function
Defining characteristic/main strength

Auxiliary Function
Sidekick to the dominant function.

Tertiary Function
Not very noticeable

Inferior Function
Least noticeable

Not only do we have to look at what functions we have, but we also have to look at what order they are in. They are organized by how strong they are or how conscious they are. The strongest one is the dominant function. It is followed by auxiliary, tertiary, and inferior.

The dominant function is the defining characteristic of your personality type. It's what makes you tick at your core and what you use the most. When you are doing something that uses this function fully, you will feel like your most authentic self. This activity will energize you and make you feel the most alive. The auxiliary function can be just as strong as the dominant one if it is developed enough. It usually works hand in hand with the dominant function as an assistant or sidekick.

The tertiary and inferior functions are much less developed and noticeable, however, they still make up an important part of our personality.

INFJ Functional Stack

Dominant: Introverted Intuition (Ni)

Auxiliary: Extroverted Feeling (Fe)

Tertiary: Introverted Thinking (Ti)

Inferior: Extroverted Sensing (Se)

Our personality develops based on our functional stack. The first thing we notice when we are young is our Introverted Intuition (Ni), that ability to just know things. We also notice our Extroverted Feeling (Fe). This leads us to know how others feel and be concerned about what they think and the general harmony of those around us. Our Introverted Intuition (Ni) and Extroverted Feeling (Fe) work well together. We can see things that most people don't and read underlying motives pretty easily.

When we are young, we are quick to express the things we feel and see. This can lead to people accusing us of being judgmental or seeing things too narrowly, especially because we are so sure of what we know and so quick to come to those decisions. We have a tendency to take these accusations straight to heart and question our intuition and feeling functions.

A young INFJ will not understand that not everyone thinks how we do or understands things how we do. It usually takes time and a lot of criticism and heartbreak before we see that we shouldn't be so open with our knowledge and opinions.

As we grow up, we notice our Extroverted Sensing (Se) more. This inferior function fights with the dominant function at the worst time in our lives, right around the time we are going to high school and college. Nearly all INFJs struggle so much to find their purpose in life, which is usually associated with their career and/or life partner. They want to find the right thing and make sure they don't mess it up. Unfortunately, our Extroverted Sensing (Se) causes us to make some questionable choices in our career and our relationships, just at the time when we are making these big decisions.

Eventually, we also notice our Introverted Thinking (Ti) function. We use this function to stop the fighting between our Introverted Intuition (Ni) and our Extroverted Sensing (Se). It helps us to find balance and make better judgments.

A lot of INFJs only develop their personalities to this point. It satisfies them with what they know and have no desire to move forward or understand more.

Some INFJs, however, are constantly searching to know more about themselves and how they operate. They learn continuously until they can no longer. With learning comes awareness and the ability to improve the less noticed functions, to bring them to light and know how to use them to our advantage. This personal growth will lead us to that purpose we long for and that feeling of being whole.

Dominant: Introverted Intuition (Ni)

The dominant function for INFJs is Introverted Intuition (Ni). As we discussed in chapter 3, Intuition in the ability to know things. Because this is mostly a subconscious process and because most people don't experience intuition, it's often seen as something magical or spiritual. INFJs are thought of as prophets or fortune-tellers.

The process of Introverted Intuition is not magic at all, however, it's of a simple process. INFJs use our Inferior function, Extroverted Sensing, to observe what is going on around us in great detail. We notice everything. Through this observation, we collect all kinds of information and organize it in our minds. We are constantly looking for patterns and connections to make it all make sense. We then take these patterns and apply them to future scenarios to "predict the future."

Most people who have intuition experience this process on a subconscious level. It really isn't noticeable. They know that they just know things, but they don't know how they know. An underdeveloped or young INFJ will feel the same way.

However, as we get older and become more aware of the process, we see what is going on in real-time. We notice that we are noticing things and making connections between them. It's not always at the front of our minds, so we do still experience the phenomenon of just knowing something, but we also understand how it works and trust the process more.

Auxiliary: Extroverted Feeling (Fe)

The auxiliary function for INFJs is Extroverted Feeling (Fe). This function helps us to relate to others. Since the function is extroverted, meaning it's directed outwards, we are more concerned with the thoughts and feelings of others than we are with our own thoughts and feelings.

This function makes us great peacemakers and negotiators. Working with our Introverted Intuition and Extroverted Sensing, we can notice the feelings of others and determine how best to understand, relate to and help them. Many people feel that INFJs can understand them better than they can understand themselves.

It's a lot more difficult for INFJs to notice and understand their own feelings. Because our feeling function is extroverted, we have a hard time processing our own emotions. When we are going through something difficult, we will usually turn to a trusted friend or loved one for support.

This function helps INFJs to express our feelings. Because we have such a hard time processing feelings internally, we need an outlet to process them. A lot of times we don't understand our feelings and our intuitions until we have written them down or spoken them out loud. In these times we turn to our closest friends for help and support. It's important to note that the best form of help that we need is someone to just be patient and listen to us talk. We like to get things out in the open and voice our theories and observations. We don't always need help to sort things out. Just a listening ear. It's important to our mental health and wellbeing to have this outlet.

INFJs have a tendency to be dark, with a thought pattern of being negative. Our darkness comes from years and years of being misunderstood and overlooked. It's easy for us to see ourselves as the victim and be pessimistic about the future. We are more likely to voice these feelings around our closest friends while keeping a more pleasant tone with those we don't know.

The dominant and auxiliary functions are often at odds with each other for INFJs. Our Introverted Intuition wants us to stay true to our values and our internal harmony, while our Extroverted Feeling is only concerned with pleasing others. When one of our friends asks us to do something that violates our values, we will often do it to make our friend happy and keep the peace, all the while beating ourselves up inside for betraying our values.

It's important for INFJs to listen to our intuition and do what feels right to us, rather than betray our values for someone else. Our intuition guides us through our life, and when we ignore it, we feel lost and confused. People in our lives will come and go, but we have to live with ourselves forever.

Tertiary: Introverted Thinking (Ti)

The third function for INFJs, also called the Tertiary function, is Introverted Thinking (Ti). This function brings some reasoning to our minds. It helps us navigate our intuitions and feelings from a logical perspective. INFJs are often said to use both the thinking and feeling sides of their brains. This is true, especially for more developed INFJs who use their Introverted Thinking to keep their other functions in check.

The downside of Introverted Thinking is that it can cause us to doubt our intuitions and our feelings. It causes us to look for a logical reason for these feelings or solid proof before we can trust them. As we grow and learn more about our personality, we recognize this pattern and find a way for all the functions to work together, rather than against each other.

Inferior: Extroverted Sensing (Se)

The last INFJ function is the Inferior function, Extroverted Sensing (Se). The inferior function is the least used and is often unconscious or even repressed. It takes work and development to use it effectively.

Extroverted Sensing is the ability to be present, to notice the things around you and pay attention to the details. INFJs have great difficulty being in the present. We live for our Introverted Intuition and thoroughly enjoy being in that space. We don't even notice what is going on around us. We are so deep in thought and processing that sometimes it takes a while before we notice the surrounding environment. This can be a dangerous game for us since we are highly sensitive. When we aren't paying attention to what's happening around us, we can become overstimulated without even noticing.

Anything that has to do with sensing can overwhelm us. We stay away from new things, places, foods, smells, because they can overwhelm us easily. However, it's important for us to tap into this function from time to time and enjoy the surrounding things and to take a break from what's going on inside our heads.

7

Strengths

INFJs have some amazing and wonderful strengths. We are often seen as magical and mysterious, yet oh so rare. We can understand others so thoroughly that they are blown away by our knowledge of them. They long to be seen in such a deep way. So many of us end up as counselors to our friends and family members, helping them to work through their deepest thoughts and concerns. We're the negotiator at work and at home, always striving to keep the peace.

We are thoughtful planners who know what's coming and how best to prepare for it. We've been planning our dreams for years. There's a deep determination that drives us forward in those dreams to make sure they become a reality.

It's a bit of a mystery how someone so calm and sweet can also be so direct and assertive. That's just one of those classic INFJ traits though: all or nothing, black or white and somehow both at the same time.

Insightful

INFJs have an amazing intuition that is active all the time. It operates without us even realizing what's happening. We analyze things in the background of our minds and come to conclusions about people and situations quickly. We see how things are connected, the big picture with all the little details and how all of it works together.

We can see right through people quickly. We see their motives and desires. We get feelings about what kind of person they are and how they operate. Manipulation and lies don't work on us most of the time, because we can see straight through it.

Our intuition also gives us the ability to sort through problems quickly. We're always looking for how things work, how they are connected and the why behind the problem. We see the structure and the cause and effect. We use our insights to see exactly what's the creative and efficient ways to fix the problems.

Fortune telling

OK, we can't see the future, not in a magical way. But we use our intuition to see patterns in people and situations and then use that knowledge to predict what will happen. It's sometimes shocking how close we can get and how often we are right.

Not only is it true that history repeats itself, but people repeat the same things repeatedly. It takes seeing those patterns, recognizing them and then imagining future events with that knowledge to see what's coming. For INFJs, most of this happens unconsciously. We do it so frequently and so fluid that we don't even notice what's going on.

This is an amazing talent to have, but it can get us into trouble. When these predictions are expressed too openly, we risk being called judgmental or jumping to conclusions. Some people may accuse us of being closed-minded. This happened to me a lot when I was younger, and I never understood why. I could see the situation, so why didn't other people understand?

I realized that the answer was in my question. They don't understand because they don't see things like we do. Not everyone has intuition as a part of their personality. In fact, only INFJs and INTJs have Introverted Intuition as the dominant function in their functional stack. ENFJs and ENTJs have it as their auxiliary function, which is like the assistant to the dominant function. That means only 7.9% of the population use this function like we do. No wonder they don't understand, right?

Planning

Our intuition, with the ability it gives us to see patterns and connections, makes us amazing planners! We think through so many scenarios in our heads constantly that we understand what will probably happen, what could happen, and about a hundred other contingencies. We see the big picture of the situation. We can make plans that are flexible enough to work in those possibilities and change them on the fly because we're already prepared.

We are also great planners because we think about others. One person's plan can affect so many people. Through looking at the whole plan and the bigger picture, we're able to see the connections and the effects our plans will have on other people. We consider their needs and wants and plan to suit everyone.

Decisive

We use our intuition and planning abilities to put our dreams and goals into action. We can come up with a plan, think it through, and then put it to work. We can be very decisive about what we want and how we will get it. We can see the whole situation, no matter how complex. We know what steps we need to take to get to what we want. We'll break it down and start the process. And we have the determination to see it through to the end.

Determined

When an INFJ sets their mind to do something, they will pursue it with a passion and determination that will astonish even their closest friends. We are not afraid to dream big dreams and put in the work to accomplish them. INFJs are also not afraid to stand up for what we believe in. This doesn't always sit well with those around us, but we rarely let that hold us back. When we set our minds to do something, we get it done.

Understanding

INFJs have an amazing ability to understand people. We are natural empaths who see people as they are. It's so easy for us to imagine ourselves in their position and see what they are going through, whether it's sadness or pain. We get it, even if we haven't even experienced it ourselves. Our heart goes out to them and we long to ease their pain in whatever way we can.

This gift is so much stronger for our friends and family. We can feel their feelings and emotions as if they were our own. When they come to us for comfort, they don't get placation or a simple response. We put ourselves in their pain and strive to help them with a thoughtful and meaningful response. We want them to know that we care about them and do whatever we can to help them realize that we understand and that we genuinely care about them.

The counselor

Because of our response to their pain, we often become the counselor to our friends and family. They know that we will listen to whatever problem they have. We'll provide an understanding and insight into their worries without judging them for their thoughts or actions. We'll help them see more sides to the matter and come up with the best course of action.

We use our intuition to guide us through their concerns and our extroverted sensing to see all the details. We see the pig picture and connect all the dots together, providing our counselee with information they hadn't considered or a solution that they couldn't see.

The negotiator

We love peace. That's our happy place. We place so much value on it that when something or someone is disturbing that peace, we'll get in the middle of it and see how we can help. Because we see so many sides to situations and can see the big picture, we are excellent negotiators. We are fair in our judgments, listening to both sides and seeing the advantages and disadvantages. We can also determine the best solution and present it in a way that everyone thinks' they've gotten what they wanted, and it was their own idea. As long as it restores the peace, we rarely care that much about who gets the credit. We just want everyone to be happy.

Helping others

INFJs are very skilled at understanding the needs of those around us. We use our intuition and our natural curiosity to discover these needs. Then we do whatever we can to help. We look for the people who are broken and misunderstood because we relate to those people so well. Since we grow up feeling out of place, we know how difficult that can be and want to ease this burden on anyone else. We also look for anyone who can't help themselves, like children, the elderly, or animals. We're interested in helping anyone who needs someone to be there for them. We'll show up.

Because of this desire to help, we gravitate towards the nonprofit sector of work. We like to work for a cause that benefits others. We want our work to make someone else's life better in whatever way we can.

Loyal

INFJs are loyal. Once you have us as a friend we will show up for you no matter what. We're the ones who will cancel plans because you need us. Is it 2am? We didn't notice. We dropped what we were doing because we knew you were in a difficult situation and we wanted to help.

It takes a lot to lose our loyalty. We want to be there for our people through thick and thin. We'll ride out the storm and give people more chances than we should, hoping that loyalty will be remembered and returned. But we also understand when it isn't.

Inspiring

Because we relate so well to others, we can easily determine what they need and how to motivate them. We have this amazing ability to connect with people, and we want to put it to good use. This is especially true if we are speaking about something that we enjoy and are passionate about. It shines through in our words and our actions. We speak to the core and from our hearts. We can break things down in a way that others understand and really touch them with our words.

Creative

Our creative imagination helps us to solve problems of all kinds. We can see how systems work clearly. Then we can analyze them to make sure they are efficient and effective.

We can also solve human problems like communication and misunderstandings. We are great at learning the communication style of those around us and being able to understand what they are saying and what they aren't saying. Then we can interpret it for others to resolve issues. This makes us amazing at negotiating and conflict resolution.

The chameleon

INFJs are very adaptable. We can read our environment and adapt however we need to fit in. We can relate to and understand many types of people. After observing their communication styles, we know how best to communicate with them. Once we see how they decide we can tailor how we provide information to best fit their needs. Whatever the case may be, we are flexible enough to fit in just about anywhere.

Wrap up

Our strengths make up a huge part of our personality. A lot of them boil down to our Introverted Intuition and Extroverted Feeling. Being able to see the bigger picture, to know things that most people don't and to feel the feelings of others gives us such an advantage in so many areas. We can connect to people in such an extraordinary way. We can make them feel seen and heard and understood so well, which is really what most people are missing in their lives today.

Our strengths drive us to be of service to the world in whatever way we can. We want to serve people, to help them be the best version of themselves. We know what a valuable skill that is and how much the world needs us.

My biggest strength is my ability to really see people and get to their truth, something I think that helps me connect with others as a life and relationship coach.

Sarah Woehler, INFJ Relationship Coach

My favorite thing about being an INFJ is that I can connect easily with all different kinds of people. This skill has gotten me friends all over the world, some of whom I keep in touch with for decades. It's also allowed me to professionally network well. Complete strangers have given me career advice and really helped me out because I'm good at authentically connecting.

Bryn Bonino, Branding Strategist

My biggest strength as an INFJ is my emotional intelligence. It gives me the gift of knowing what people are thinking and feeling without them ever having to tell me. Then I can easily shift my energy to their needs.

Laura Charelle, Health Coach

INFJs bring authenticity, depth, and intensity to their relationships. They add texture and nuance to conversations by mirroring profound insights others hadn't thought of previously.

Gabrielle Valdes, Relationship Coach

8

Weaknesses

Most of the time, INFJs are portrayed to be sweet and happy people who are always there to help those around them. That's not always true. We have a dark and twisty side that comes out from time to time. Sometimes we get stuck in situations that leave us spiraling through our emotions with seemingly no way out. Or we take on too much because we want to save the world and can see clearly how we can, but we get burnt out.

It's important for us to recognize the areas of our personality that are not so strong, not to beat ourselves up, but to understand ourselves better. Some of these things may be things that we need to improve on. Others we may just need to be aware of and accept. It's completely up to you how to handle them.

Extremely private

INFJs are private people. We have a knack for making people feel comfortable and adapting to the surrounding people. But that means we end up hiding our real personality and feelings to make others feel better. We hide how we feel and what we think to keep the peace and keep those around us happy.

We get so used to putting on a front for our friends and we are so good at it they may not even know who we really are. Decide for yourself how big of a problem this is for you. If it's your coworker who you rarely see outside of work, does it really matter who they think you are? Maybe not. But if it's your friends, family and significant other, that can be a much bigger problem that needs to be confronted.

We also have very strong and deep emotions that we dislike to share with others. We protect these feelings fiercely to protect ourselves. Most of us have been hurt repeatedly from sharing our emotions, so we've learned to keep them to ourselves.

Difficulty making friends

INFJs have problems making new friends. It's hard for us to find people we connect with where there is a mutual connection. Most people don't understand us. Only 2 of the MBTI personality types have Introverted Intuition as a dominant function (INFJ & INTJ) and 2 have it as an auxiliary function (ENFJ & ENTJ). That means only 4 types will really understand what drives us the most!

We also have to consider how many personality types have Intuition at all. Half of the MBTI types have Intuition as a preference, but those eight types only make up 27% of the population. That means that 73% of the people you meet won't understand what intuition is because they don't use it in their everyday lives. When you break it down further to just the types who have Introverted Intuition as a dominant or auxiliary function, that's only 7.9% of the population. No wonder we are so misunderstood![9]

People who don't understand our intuition don't see things the way we do. They don't want to talk about the deep things that we enjoy talking about and exploring. We have a problem meeting them

Personality Type Distribution in the General Population

Intuitive

ENFP	8.1
INFP	4.4
INTP	3.3
ENTP	3.2
ENFJ	2.5
INTJ	2.1
ENTJ	1.8
INFJ	1.5
Total	26.9

Sensing

ISFJ	13.8
ESFJ	12.3
ISTJ	11.6
ISFP	8.8
ESTJ	8.7
ESFP	8.5
ISTP	5.4
ESTP	4.3
Total	73.4

Source: MBTI published by CPP

at surface level topics. It's a constant struggle for us to find friends who understand us, even just a little.

Meeting new people is a challenge. While we are a good judge of character right off the bat, we take a while to open up to new people regardless of how we feel about them. We want to get to know them first and see what kind of person they are. We mold what we show them of our personality to meet their response and their needs. It's a long and complicated process for us to really open up and show someone our true self.

Manipulative

Through getting to know people, we adapt our personality to fit what they need. It's an unconscious and unintentional manipulation on our part. We want to be the best friend to this new person in our lives, so we give them what we think they want and need, but we hide the rest of ourselves. They go on thinking we are a different person than what we really are.

Sensitive

Whether or not we like to admit it, INFJs are sensitive. We take other's words straight to heart, especially criticism. We are quick to shut down in the face of conflict just to process what we are thinking and feeling. When we're pushed too far, our reaction can be very un-characteristic of our normal personality. Our responses can be sharp and brutal because of an attack on our values.

This is where the manipulation is a problem. We've told our friend we are one way and when we get pushed too far, we lash out and show them how mean we can be in one foul swoop. They are left feeling lost and confused because they did not understand how we really are. We feel hurt as well they didn't understand us at all and most of the time we're confused why they don't understand us. We walk away from them, hurt and rejected, feeling like no one will ever understand us.

Need lots of alone time

As empaths, INFJs soak up the feelings and emotions of those around us. We take on these things and our own. The way we process these feelings is by spending time alone. We need time to sort things out and figure out how we really feel before we can present it to anyone else.

We chose to spend a lot of time alone though because this is how we recharge. Being around people drains our energy and we need to build it back up before we can go out into the world again. All of this alone time can lead to broken friendships if we are not careful. Not everyone understands and respects our need to be alone. It's important that we communicate what's think about others in these situations.

Shutting down

When INFJs get overwhelmed with life or emotions, we have a tendency to just shut down. It takes a while to process things, and we need time and space to do that. Unfortunately, we don't always communicate what we are doing. We are known among our friends to just disappear from time to time. During these processing times, we just want to be alone, to figure things out for ourselves. This time could be days, weeks or even months depending on what we are dealing with.

Not asking for help

INFJs can use both sides of our brains, the creative side, and the logical side. We have a very active imagination and an amazing intuition. We also have a natural ability to figure things out for ourselves, and we are superb at it. So, when we get into difficult situations, we think we can figure everything out all by ourselves. We try to figure things out, sometimes prevailing, but sometimes making them a lot worse. Often we have to get to the very, very end of our rope before we will reach out for help. Sometimes these situations would be a lot easier if we would just ask someone for help a lot sooner.

All or nothing

When we do something, it is all or nothing. There is no balance and no in-between. We commit ourselves to projects 100% and dedicate all of our time and energy to making them a reality. But this can get us into some serious trouble. We can become so obsessed with something that we block everything else out and neglect things that we should do instead.

Brutal honesty

INFJs have a unique way of looking at the world. We are honest and straightforward in our communication style. Sometimes we don't even understand how honest we are until we see the shocked looks on the faces of the people we are talking to. This honesty is in sharp contrast to the feelings of others and the concern we hold for them.

Pushing through the pain

Whether or not we like to admit it, INFJs are sensitive. It doesn't take much to shake us to our core. What's worse, we are so concerned about the people around us feeling bad that we don't tell them how they have hurt us. We keep our poker face in place and push through the pain, blaming ourselves for being hurt by what they said to us.

We are great at keeping things to ourselves, too good in fact. It's hard for us to open up to anyone because they have misunderstood us for years. So we hold it all in, thinking there is no one that will understand, anyway. Why even try?

Eventually, there is too much inside and it all comes out. The explosions don't happen often, but when they do, they are big! Everything we have been holding in for months and months comes out in one massive explosion. It can be a scary experience! The good news is it only happens once or twice a year.

Feeling hopeless

INFJs have amazing imaginations. We love to spend time there thinking about and planning for the future. Sometimes these dreams are impossible, and we are reasonable enough to understand this. It leads to a feeling of hopelessness, missing something that never even existed.

High Expectations

We have high expectations for ourselves. We are constantly looking for ways to make things better and see all the places that we can be better. We strive to be the best at everything that we do. It's easy for us to let those expectations get out of control and the result is being hard on ourselves.

Perfectionistic

We like things to be perfect. We spend a lot of time in our heads imagining the perfect future down to the smallest detail. When reality doesn't match up to that vision, it can be hard for us to deal with.

We also get stuck in planning mode. We don't want to start a project until we have it perfectly planned out and know exactly how it will turn out. This tendency leaves us with lots of plans and not nearly as many actions.

Expecting too much of others

Not only do we expect a lot out of ourselves, but we expect a lot out of the surrounding people. It's not on the same level as what we expect from ourselves, but it is high. And the more respect that we have for them, the higher the position that they hold, the more we expect out of them. We look at what we would do in their situation and don't understand why they aren't capable of doing something similar.

OK, that was rough...

In the beginning of this chapter it's important for us to recognize our weaknesses, but not dwell on them. We can't be good at everything, unfortunately. But when you know where your weaknesses are, you can adapt how you operate to make the most of the things. You don't have to set out on a quest to fix these things. Don't make that your next obsession. Sometimes knowing about the issue is enough to work around it when you need to.

My biggest strength is my ability to really see people and get to their truth, something I think that helps me connect with others as a life and relationship coach. Ironically, my strength probably presents as a weakness at times in that I feel people's energies and experiences so intensely that it can take a toll by leaving me tapped out at times. I find ways of resetting by exercise, meditation, and ad hoc therapy sessions which is instrumental to further growth for me as well.

Sarah Woehler, INFJ Relationship Coach

The downside of being an INFJ is that we tend to be highly sensitive and empaths. This is good in many ways, but sometimes the world seems to be too much. I can get overwhelmed in intense situations and my energy will drain. This intense ability to feel also means that I fight for what I believe in. This pushes some people away.

But honestly, I think the world would be a nicer place if more leaders were highly sensitive and empathic INFJs. I'm proud of who I am, and I'm glad I'm an INFJ.

Bryn Bonino, Branding Strategist

My biggest weakness as an INFJ is deeply feeling everyone else's emotions. At times it can be hard to separate someone else's feelings to my own, which can cause a lot of internal stress and fatigue.

Laura Charelle, Health Coach

INFJs might believe that they have to do things alone. Others might perceive them as secretive, but really they're waiting for people to show that they care. For an INFJ to be successful, they must know that there are people out there who will reciprocate what they need.

Gabrielle Valdes, Relationship Coach

9

Communication

INFJs are often portrayed as skilled and prolific communicators, but that's not always the case. Most times we struggle to put the complicated web of thoughts, connections and patterns that we see into words that others understand. What comes out of our mouth is actually a mess of half-finished sentences as we hastily try to rework our thoughts into something more simple and understandable.

Writing is usually a better option for us as we're able to slow down and think about what we really want to say. When we see our words in front of us, they make more sense.

There's a huge learning curve for young INFJs to think about those around them in terms of how much they know about us. Once we understand the people, we're talking to and their level of understanding of us, then we can really become effective at communicating with them.

The bigger picture

We have spoken about many areas of our personality that lead us to understand people on a deep level. Our intuition gives us such an accurate picture of them we can understand them even better than they understand themselves.

We spoke in Chapter 8 about how only 2 of the MBTI personality types have Introverted Intuition as a dominant function (INFJ & INTJ) and 2 have it as an auxiliary function (ENFJ & ENTJ). That means only 4 types will really understand what drives us the most. Those 4 types only make up 7.9% of the population. When we start with that knowledge, it's easier to see why we are misunderstood so much![10]

Personality Type Distribution in the General Population

Intuitive Personality Types
Thinking & Feeling

ENFJ	2.5%
INTJ	2.1%
ENTJ	1.8%
INFJ	1.5%
Total	7.9%

Source: MBTI published by CPP

It took me years to understand this. When I was young, I thought everyone saw the world as I did. I thought everyone had intuition and a natural understanding of people and the big picture of life and the world. I would get into situations at school or work where I was

10 steps ahead of everyone else and it lost them completely. How could they not see what was right in front of them? It just made little sense to me.

I was working with a former boss of mine who used to belittle me a lot. We would talk about a project that I needed to work on, and my mind would start flying through all the details and coming up with questions that were 50 steps and 6 months down the road. I saw the whole project as crystal clear right from the start. When I would voice these questions, my boss would get mad at me and tell me I wasn't paying attention to what he was saying. Then he would launch into repeating step one of the project again.

I would get so mad! "Why is he treating me like I'm stupid?" I would fume internally as he repeated step one for a third time.

Through many of these exchanges it finally dawned on me he was so focused on step one because he couldn't see step 50. He didn't want to talk about what would happen 6 months down the road because he did not think things through like I did. He could only see what was right in front of him. He would get mad and me and belittle me because I had an ability that he didn't have and he didn't want to look bad in front of me.

Because my boss had a sensing preference, he couldn't tap into intuition. He didn't know how. It wasn't a part of his makeup. It's important to realize that because neither one of us was doing anything wrong at the beginning of the conversation. He was looking at classic sensing, and I was looking at 6 months from now, classic intuition. But you have to step back and understand that to communicate effectively.

Other people only understand us to their level of understanding. 73% of people don't have Intuition as a preference. That means that they only develop their intuition to a 10-year-old's level of understanding. It could be as low as a 3-year-old's level of understanding. Can you imagine trying to explain to a 3-year-old what intuition is? I can't![11]

How INFJs communicate

The inside of an INFJ's head is an interesting place. It's a complicated web of pictures, details, stories, movies, facts, ideas, memories and theories all woven together to connect. The connections come from many places and. Sometimes they are blatant and obvious to any observer, but most of the time they are a lot deeper and more obscure. We are constantly running through ideas, theories and patterns to understand things on the deepest level possible. We love to be lost in thought in a quiet, peaceful place with snacks close by.

There's nothing like someone who stands in front of us wanting to chat and ruin such a blissful state.

When we communicate, we are quiet at first. We want to know what you are thinking and feeling. It's an information-gathering process. We base our response off of you. You tell us how to be around you. To know that we have to start with listening and observing. We'll be quiet while we're reading people and planning our response.

When we know the person we're talking to, we're a lot more comfortable from the beginning. We already know what they are expecting from us, so we need not be as quiet. However, we still adapt how we communicate with them based on what we know they are comfortable with. We are constantly reading their responses through their words, facial expressions, body language, tone of voice, etc. Always collecting and analyzing information. What's most important is what's not said. We'll analyze that too. This all happens in a flash as the conversation goes on. Constantly reading and adapting to the environment.

Part of our reason for reading people so much is our determining of what information to share about ourselves. We don't like anyone to know too much about us. That's a dangerous game that we've all been burned on before. Our thoughts, feelings and ideas are so important to us we want to protect them. They aren't for all to see.

When we open up a little, we're even more aware of how the other person is reacting and responding. Our need for control is high here and obvious when looked at logically.

We also measure our communication to make sure that our responses are understandable. INFJs are notorious for not talking about an idea or theory for months and then unloading a thesis on an unsuspecting victim. Once we understand this about ourselves, it's a lot easier to keep it in check.

Communication style

INFJs have Extroverted Sensing, which makes us so aware of the thoughts and feelings of those around us. Most of the time this is present in our minds when we voiced our opinion about something. We measure their feelings and craft our words to make them comfortable and happy. At the very least, we don't want them to be upset. We know how to give people what they want and are more than happy to do that.

Sometimes our communication is soft and thoughtful, but there are also times when we are much more direct. Because we understand those around us so well, we can use that knowledge to our advantage when we need to. If our intention is to inflict pain, we can craft our point to cause a dire amount of pain with the least amount of effort. This isn't something that we enjoy, but when it needs to be done we'll step up and do it.

I'll write you a letter

INFJs are much more effective at communicating through writing. When writing something down, we're able to slow our thought process down and think about the important points that we want to make. We're able to see it in front of us and know what's important and helpful and what just needs to go.

When we get stuck with trying to communicate something, it's helpful to write it down, even if it's just in a journal that only you can see. It will help to organize our thoughts before we put them out there in the world.

How to relate to others more effectively

As INFJs, one of our strong suits is meeting people where they are. We like to understand them and adapt to how they understand. That is the best thing you can do when communicating with someone with a sensing preference. But that means you have to tap into your sensing and try to develop it more, so you can relate to them effectively.

How to manage conflict

There's a big difference between relating to people on their level and giving into what they want. Let me tell you a story about something that happened to me recently.

I have this problem where all of my friends seem to leave me. Not always right away, but at some point, they all leave. It's like there's an expiration date on all of my friendships. Does this happen to you too, or is it just me?

It's hard enough for me to make friends because I'm different from most people. I'm quiet and shy when you first meet me and awkward too, usually. Plus, I don't like people and I don't like small talk. There's so much of that involved in new people, too. I just avoid it.

Then, when I go through this whole process of meeting someone new, eventually the whole thing blows up anyway and they leave. So why bother? I'd rather deal with being lonely than go through the process only to be disappointed every time.

I never understood why this happened. I looked at it from every angle I could imagine, but couldn't come up with an answer. Then something else happened, and the answer smacked me right in the face. It all comes back to communication.

Let me tell you a story...

I was looking for an apartment during the summer of 2019. Renting an apartment in Boston, MA, where I live, is unbelievably expensive. Decent apartments for reasonable prices are hard to find. Somehow I found one, just South of the city, that was oceanfront and gorgeous! I will do anything to get it.

The landlord was a woman in her late 50s who I could tell was looking for a daughter. She said things like, "If you get sick I'll bring you some soup!" and "We should go to dinner!" I knew she wanted more than a tenant, but I overlooked it and signed the lease, anyway.

Almost right away she started coming into my apartment without telling me, moving my things around, opening my mail and so many other inappropriate things. Instead of me speaking up and saying, "it really makes me uncomfortable when you come into my apartment when I'm not there," I didn't. I didn't want to make her mad or do anything to rock the boat, so I just kept quiet.

But all too soon it got to where I couldn't ignore it anymore, and I moved. She turned on me quickly, as I just knew she would. She threatened to call her lawyer and said I owed her the full rent for the remaining lease, close to $8,000.

I told her, "Cool. Call your lawyer. I'll call mine and we'll figure this thing out." Then I went to work searching through the Massachusetts rental laws and found about 10 things she had done that had violated and voided the lease long before I had left. I pointed them all out to her in a very cold and matter-of-fact way, which differed completely from the way I had spoken to her before.

Her response was something like this, "You are NOT the person I thought you were! Why are you treating me this way and being so nasty? What's wrong with you?"

I took this as a personal attack on me and my personality. It deeply hurt my feelings, even though I didn't care at all about her feelings for me. She had done what so many other people, bosses & friends, have done to me in the past: tell me that there was something wrong with my personality. That I was not OK and that I needed to change.

The epiphany

I was so hurt I recalled the story to one of my good friends. She's straightforward in her communication, but sometimes it's necessary in order for me to get the point. She said that she didn't know why I was so surprised because this always happens to me, not just in this situation, but with all of my friends. I agreed that it does happen a lot and said I do not understand why.

She had all the answers. She said, "The problem is you tell people what they want to hear. You act like everything is ok and never tell them there's a problem. But then, when you've finally had enough, your real personality comes out, and they are dazed and confused because you are TRULY NOT the person they thought you were."

I couldn't believe my ears. The answer had been right in front of me the whole time, and somehow I missed it.

Here's the problem

Let's break it down a little more, because this is a whole thing. As INFJs, we have this AMAZING ability to intuitively know what others want and need. It's one of my favorite things about being INFJ, but if we aren't careful, it can get us into trouble quickly.

Let me give you an example. Let's say you meet someone new and you like them. You admire their work, and you enjoy their personality. You really want to get to know them more. So you set to work trying to figure out ways you can connect with them. You figure out what they like and don't like. You find any angle you can to get to know them.

And then you give them everything they want. They want to eat at a Thai restaurant? COOL! You're game... even though you hate Thai food. They want to go to a trendy new coffee shop? AWESOME!! You're all about it... even though you'd much rather have Starbucks. They want to see that new superhero movie that everyone just loves? YEAH! You stand in line with them for hours to get tickets... even though you hate those movies and people and being at the movies with people.

The list goes on and on. It's one thing after another and before you know it you've created a whole new personality for this new friend. You don't even recognize yourself when you're around them.

The spiral

You think about telling them the truth, but you know they wouldn't understand. You're SO FAR from who you are that they wouldn't want to be friends with you. You know that you have nothing in common with them, but you want to have a friend and you think this is the only way that you can have friends. All of your friends are like this, so that must be true.

Then... you take it personally. You think no one will ever like your real personality because no one you know knows the real you and why would they want to? You don't fit in with them and you know that you wouldn't if they knew the real you. It's like a cycle that just keeps repeating itself. The only solution you can come up with is that it's your personality that's broken and messed up because you're not like everyone else. I felt this way for years. I kept up the cycle and kept blaming myself, and it just got worse and worse.

The answer

So then we go back to my friend who says, "It's YOU. YOU'RE THE PROBLEM. You're doing this to yourself!" At first, it really hurt me when she said that. Why was she being so mean?!? It's not me! It's my awful personality and I can't change that!

Then I started thinking about it more. It's not that my personality is awful or wrong or broken. It's not that at all. There is NOTHING wrong with my personality. The problem is me. It's how I act around my friends. It's the fact that I want to be friends with them SO BADLY that I unintentionally manipulate them. I lead them to believe that I'm someone that I'm not because I think that's the only way they'll like me. I've believed that there is something wrong with my personality for so long that I convinced myself that I had to be someone else in order for anyone to like me.

I bet you do the same thing. Whether you take it to the same extreme as I did is another question. I hope not. But if you do, there is hope!! I found the answer. But I have to warn you–it will hurt, and it's difficult.

Are you ready?

Stop being fake. It stings.... Doesn't it? As INFJs, we pride ourselves on how real and authentic we are. We love being genuine and deep. We think of ourselves in a "real" light. And we despise fake people. I know that's a strong word, but it's accurate for me. I hate to admit that I'm fake because I don't like people who are that way.

And there's another epiphany... Do you know how you can't stand people who have the problems you are trying to overcome? Well... maybe that's why we don't like fake people so much. We can relate to them too well.

Stop being fake

How do we stop being fake? This is the real question. It's difficult, and it takes work. The first step is having the awareness of what you are doing and admitting you do it. That's hard. Don't discount the effort you have to put into doing that. It's a lot.

The next step is hard too. It's changing your behavior. It's recognizing what you are doing in real-time and making a different decision. Instead of saying, "Yeah, I'm cool with Thai food." Say, "No, actually I don't like Thai food at all. Can we go somewhere else?"

I will not lie to you: not all of your friends will be OK with your newfound ability to ask for what you want and need. In fact, a lot of them might not be OK at all. They could have the same reaction as my former landlord. They might say things like, "You're not the person I thought you were!" And it's true. You're not. And it's also OK that you're not. Those people will walk away from you, and that's hard, but it's OK. They are not your people.

Your real and true friends will want you to speak up and will welcome your opinion. They will be perfectly fine with your new desire to tell them how you really feel. If you find that many people leave you, it's OK. It's hard, but it's OK. You are just making room in your life for new friends who will value your personality from the start.

We need to talk things out to understand them

I want to point out one other thing about that story. Remember that it was my friend who solved my problem for me? I've noticed that when I get stressed and confused about a big decision or something big happening in my life, I turn to all of my friends and ask their opinion. It's almost like I can't decide until I talk it out.

As INFJs, we have problems sorting out how we feel about things. That's our Extroverted Feeling coming out. We are so busy looking at everyone else that we can't see ourselves. We need to get our ideas out of our head somehow to process them better. Sometimes journaling is perfect for this. When I see the words on paper in front of me, they seem to make more sense. Sometimes, though, it takes talking about the issue before it makes sense to me. I can't tell you how many times I've come to a huge life epiphany from talking to my niece or one of my friends.

When you struggle with communicating

There are several things that you can do to get better at communicating with others.

Understand that your mind works differently than most others

It's difficult to explain some connections we see. I used to get really confused why people don't see the same thing, but then I realized that seeing these connections is one of those superpowers that is reserved for a select few personalities, INFJ included.

As INFJs, we are constantly observing and analyzing things and making connections that most other people aren't able to make. Because of this, we can almost predict the future based on these observations. Not everyone will understand this, or believe it, even after they have seen it in action and especially if they have a sensing type of personality. But that's OK. They don't have to. You should remember that people will only understand you up to their level of understanding. It's hard for them to understand something that they have never experienced. But we, as INFJs, can meet them on their level and do our best to see where they are coming from too.

Know who you are talking to

One of the best things you can do to improve your communication is to "type" the person you are talking to or figure out what type of personality they have. It's easy to get a rough guess if you know a little about them. You only need to answer 4 questions:

1. How do they recharge?

- Do they like to spend a lot of time alone? Then they are probably an introvert.
- Do they like to spend a lot of time with other people? Then they are probably an extrovert.

2. How do they see the world?

- Are they focused on the present? Do they take everything you say at face value? They are probably a sensing type.
- Are they always talking about their plans? Are they able to understand more than just what you say? They are probably an intuitive type.

3. How do they decide?

- Do they use facts and logic to decide? They are probably a thinking type.
- Do they go with their gut feeling or what they want more than what seems practical? They are probably a feeling type.

4. How do they show the world their decisions?

- Are they organized and decisive about what they want? They are probably a judging type.
- Are they laid back and go with the flow when deciding, or more messy and relaxed? They are probably a perceiving type.

The answers to these questions will in no way give you an accurate type, but they will give you a rough guess of what type they are. Once you have a rough guess, you can look up how that type communicates. This way you can meet them on their level.

Your communication problem may be something as simple as you are very direct in your communication and they are indirect. Or you could come from an emotional place while they are more logical and objective. Once you are armed with that knowledge, you will know how to communicate in a way that they understand getting your point across.

Research your own communication

Most INFJs love learning about themselves and improving. If you haven't already, dive into how INFJs communicate, look at your strengths to see what you do well and look at your weaknesses to see where you may lack and may need to improve.

Make sure you are paying attention when you are trying to communicate, and it seems like you are failing. This is a great time to think about what works and what doesn't. Also, don't forget that it will differ from one person to another, even if they have the same personality type. We are all different, even all INFJs.

Know what you are feeling before you begin

Sometimes our communication gets jumbled because we don't know what we're trying to say. As empaths, we take on emotions and feelings from others that can get mixed up with our own thoughts and feelings. We don't know what we are thinking or feeling or even who the thoughts and feelings belong to. If we don't have this sorted out, there is no way we can communicate it to others.

It's also difficult for us to communicate when we are in the middle of processing something or thinking intensely about a subject. In those times it may be best to delay the conversation until you are more prepared and in a better space in your own head.

Another option is to simply state that you are confused and overwhelmed and see if this person can help you. If it's someone you trust, this may be the best way to go. Sometimes this is the only way we can figure out what's going on inside of our heads.

Communication is hard

Communication can be hard for INFJs, but it's not impossible. It's so important to understand how you think and how you see the world to communicate effectively. Once you do that, you know what you need to do to relate to others. ANd when you have all those details about them you can make it perfect, right? Wrong. We are all imperfect humans. We all make mistakes and say things the wrong way and leave something out that was important.

As INFJs, we are very hard on ourselves most of the time. It's easy to get caught in the trap of overthinking about what you could have said differently and how the other person received and understood what you said.

The fact of the matter is that all things considered, INFJs are actually great communicators. You are probably way better at it than you think. Make sure you are giving yourself some grace and that you recognize the good things that you said and did. Once you recognize the positives, you will gain more confidence and be able to communicate even better.

10

Relationships

INFJs often struggle to find meaningful relationships. We long for deep connections and understanding from our friends and lovers, but are all too often met with a surface level response. We take our relationships seriously because we invest so much into them. We want to know everything about the people in our lives, all of their likes and dislikes, every deep thought and feeling they have and every little thing we can do to make their life even a little better.

We make our people feel seen, heard and understood. We want them to feel loved and taken care of. We want them to know how much we care about them.

Not everyone is prepared for this kind of relationship, whether it's a friendship or a romantic relationship. Some people enjoy playing on the surface and don't want to go any deeper than that. Others just aren't prepared to be seen and understood in such a profound way. Whatever the reason, it can lead to a lot of heartache on our part. However, when we find the people who like this attention and understanding, it is extraordinary!

Friends

INFJs have a notoriously difficult time making friends. We shy away from the casual connections that most people enjoy. We don't want a bunch of acquaintances in our lives that we barely know. We'd much rather have a few true friends that we connect with on a deep and authentic level. It can be difficult for us to find people who understand us to the same level that we understand them and enjoy that level of connection.

The best place to look for these deep and meaningful friendships is in the things we enjoy. We want others who share the same passions and interests as us, but you may not just run into those kinds of people in your everyday life. You may need to go looking for them. Think about the places that you really enjoy being and where you really feel like your true, authentic self. Start there. In the book club at your local coffee shop or the writing group you joined on Facebook. Look anywhere you are doing something that you love.

When we look for friends, we look for someone who is everything to us, like a soul mate. We are idealists who see things as they could be, and as we want them to be. We also have a tendency to be perfectionists, looking for someone who will check every box, who's perfect in every way. It's important for us to remember that that is a lot of ask out of one person. We are so rare that very few people will relate to us on every level. Even if you are lucky enough to connect with another INFJ, you will still see differences. Let go of the idea in your head that everything will be perfect and accept what is real. Learn to meet others halfway in your search for friends. They won't always be what you hope them to be, but they can still turn into amazing friends.

Once we find people we connect with, we are the greatest of friends. We are loyal to those we care about and very supportive of their needs and desires. One of our greatest assets is our desire to improve and we are willing and able to share this with our friends, encouraging them to be the best version of themselves. Because we understand our friends so well, we can encourage them in a way that makes the most sense to them.

As time goes by and we trust our friends more and more, we will be more comfortable opening up to them and showing them our real, true personality. That connection continues to grow into a friendship that lasts a lifetime.

Being single

INFJs take relationships seriously, and we don't like to waste our time. We know what we want and when we don't have it, we're not afraid to go it alone. We won't settle for less than we deserve, and we're more than happy being single. It takes a lot to get us away from being single. Our significant other has to be better than the peace of our normal routine and the freedom that our singleness gives us.

Many INFJs don't even consider dating or marriage until they are in their 30s. If we go back to our functions, we discussed in chapter 6, we'll remember that adolescent INFJs struggle with finding our purpose in the world. We have a war going on between our Introverted Intuition and our Extroverted Sensing that works to rip us apart. We feel a strong sense of confusion and disorientation in the world. It may take us a good ten years to figure that out.

Once we are more comfortable with ourselves as a person and more comfortable with our place in the world, we are more open to letting someone else into our life.

Dating

Dating is yet another challenge for INFJs. We long to find someone we connect with who really gets us, but we don't like any of the traditional means of dating. Dating apps are cold and superficial. Bars are usually the last place you'll find an INFJ. So where does that leave us? We want a genuine connection with a deep person. That's hard to find in dating nowadays.

The other thing is INFJs don't want to date just to date. We're not into casual things with no labels or strings. We take finding our life partner seriously and don't want to waste time with people who don't fit our list of wants and needs. We know what we want and we won't settle for anything less.

Yes, we have a list of things we desire in a partner. It may be a long list. We love to spend hours and hours dreaming up the perfect partner for ourselves. Then we spend even more time researching what the right partner for us is and thinking through each scenario. We look to other relationships around us and those on TV and in books we love for clues about what kind of relationship we want in our lives. It's like a giant puzzle that we spend countless hours on making sure it's just right. We are picky because we know what we want. We've considered all the possibilities and are convinced that our intuition and the universe will lead us to the right person at just the right time. We cannot be convinced otherwise.

When we find the right person, it's magic. Our connection is beyond imagination and worth every second that we waited for it.

INFJs have a huge advantage in dating. We understand people so well that we can see past what's fake and straight to what's real. We can make people feel comfortable with our warm and friendly approach to them and make them understand how much we really care about them.

"I think it's something that is a gift too," relationship coach Ga-brielle Valdes told me during a podcast interview, "the ability to sense someone else's needs, being able to have a deep understanding of the other person and then also to give that to another person. That is huge, especially in the dating world. I feel like it's so rare to come by a person who's so open to giving." That openness to giving makes us desirable.

The Ideal Partner Type for an INFJ

What is the best personality type match for the INFJ? I can't tell you how many times they have asked me this question. There are so many theories out there. You can find one to fit whatever you want it to be, honestly, though some are way better than others.

Opposites attract

The most accepted theory is that opposites attract. For the INFJ, this would be an ESTP. That would mean our introverted, future-focused, feeling all the feelings selves would be paired with a loud, present-minded, logical and spontaneous adventurer. (Can you tell I'm cringing just writing this?)

It's completely up to you whether you are open to that adventure. I want to cry just thinking about it. Don't send me emails and DMs about how much you love your ESTP, this is just my opinion.

Some people suggest someone who isn't so opposite, like an ENFJ or an ENTP, as long as they have the extroverted part down. There are benefits and drawbacks to this situation. The biggest benefit and drawback is the extroverted thing. Extroverts will push introverts out of their comfort zone, but they may not understand and appreciate our need to recharge. And in the grand scheme of things, that could end up being a big thing. It's all about what you want.

Samesies

Some theories say that the same personality type works well together. This could be hard for INFJs to find another INFJ because we are so rare.

The advantage of being with another INFJ is that you would understand each other so well. But the disadvantage is that you both probably have the same or at least similar weaknesses. When neither one of you wants to make a phone call or go to the grocery store because people, how does anything get done?

Oh so close

I heard another theory recently that makes sense to me. This theory says that your best match is only one off of your personality type based on the chart below. For the INFJ that means the best matches are INTP, ENFJ and INFP.

Personality Types			
ESTJ	ISTJ	ENTJ	INTJ
ESTP	ISTP	ENTP	INTP
ESFJ	ISFJ	ENFJ	INFJ
ESFP	ISFP	ENFP	INFP

For the INFJ that means the best matches are INTP, ENFJ and INFP. I love this theory actually, but we'll get to that later.

When you have only one or two letters of your type, still have a lot in common and a lot that works. You will still get a lot of understanding, but enough difference to keep things interesting.

My niece is an INTP and we get along really well. We are both introverted and intuitive, which gives us many similarities. But we think and feel things differently, and we process things differently. It's a good balance of being similar, but different. There's a lot of understanding there.

I also have a friend who is ENFJ, who I love. She has a lot of energy and excitement and is always ready to get things done. She'll just pick up the phone to make a call or even walk right up to someone and start talking... someone she doesn't even know and has no obligation to talk to! It's fascinating to watch and a little horrifying. I adore her, but only in small doses.

Just be healthy

Many people will tell you that any two types can be together as long as they're both healthy. I'm sure that's true, though I have yet to find anyone who's healthy, myself included.

I know that relationships are all about the work and effort that you put into them, but I also know that some are just naturally easier than others. Why not give yourself every advantage you can for such an important decision?

My theory

I know you've been waiting, so here goes. I'm very partial to INFPs. I have this dream, that I'm manifesting that I will meet an INFP who is ready and willing and available for a relationship. Can you hear me universe? I'm waiting... not so patiently!

Here's my thought process: INFPs are introverted, so no forced social gatherings on the regular. They are intuitive, so bring on all the deep conversations about life and meaning and depth. They also read between the lines and just know things, like we do. Also, they have all the feels too. This could get touchy, I admit. It's not a perfect plan, but that's what makes it real.

Then there's that last letter that makes all the difference. They are the spontaneity to our planning and the mess to our organization. They are also the rainbows and lightness to our dark and heavy. They can lift us up to see the good in things and people, but also sit with us in the peaceful calm, just being alone... together. Can you see the hearts in my eyes? Doesn't it sound like heaven? *sigh*

The real truth

OK, so I have to go back and say that any type can work with any type. I really believe that, even though I'm convinced I need an INFP. The key is the healthy part. And it's up to you to make sure you are in the healthiest place you can be. Any relationship will require work, maturity and communication, no matter what theory you buy into.

Love Life

That craving for connection and depth carries over into our relationships. We strive to become better people day by day, and we take that desire with us into our relationship. We want to have a connection and to keep it. It's not a destination, but the journey of constantly learning and adjusting and growing that we enjoy.

Our love and care are deep and intense for our significant other. It's not for the faint of heart. We are enthusiastic and open to learning new things, going where we haven't been before. We are passionate about our love on a level that is not easily matched.

Intimacy

One of the many ways we share a connection with our significant other is intimacy. We rarely like to be close in proximity to people, nor do we allow people to touch us, but there is a clear exception to this rule for our love. We long to be close to them and to make sure they feel loved.

I had the pleasure of interviewing Lauren White, a sexologist and an INFJ, on my podcast, The Quiet Ones.[12] I asked her the question that comes up so often when talking about INFJs and intimacy, do INFJs have a high sex drive? Here's her response:

"Rather than high sex drive, I'm gonna say we've got a high libido. I think we've got a high interest in sex and the sexual. And we have a very rich fantasy world.

"How that translates to the act of sex and being physical in sex, I don't know that it always translates. I think we are very comfortable having this rich inner world of safe fantasy and what could be possible and really getting romantic and deep intimacy and exploring the taboo. Whether we do those things is another question."

We should also include love languages into this conversation. Gary Chapman wrote a book called The 5 Love Languages, posing a theory that there are 5 different ways that people give and receive love: Words of Affirmation, Acts of Service, Receiving Gifts, Quality Time, and Physical Touch.

I asked my INFJ community on social media what their primary love language is. 60% of them said it was spending quality time with their partner. But a third of respondents said physical touch was a close second.

INFJs crave connection. We want deep intimacy. That craving is almost painful. We want someone to love us in ways that no one else has ever done, in ways we didn't even think were possible.

Like Lauren said, we spend a lot of time in our heads thinking about how we want to be loved, imagining every detail. More than just physical intimacy, we want to be seen and understood on an intellectual and emotional level. We want someone to share our thoughts and hopes and dreams with. We want someone to understand our intuition and our "knowing" of some things. We want someone who's comfortable being deep and dark.

We also crave someone that we can be ourselves with, who will enjoy our sense or humor and our need to be cautious and organized. Someone comfortable in the quiet and loves solitude.

When we feel that connection, we are the type to think about what our partner wants and give it to them. We spend more time being focused on them and making sure that they are happy than we do thinking about us. It's a blessing and a curse. But what really makes us happy is knowing that our partner is satisfied and feels loved.

Door Slam

INFJs give and give and give in relationships. We are mostly OK with this as long as they reciprocate it in some small way. When it's not, and we feel taken advantage of, we become deeply hurt. We will try everything we know to fix the situation and save the relationship. We put our problem-solving abilities to work and try everything we can think of to make things work. Everything.

But there is a line. There is a point where enough is enough. There is a point where we get betrayed or taken advantage of too much and we respond in a cold and deliberate way, often called the door-slam.

The door-slam is an INFJ, cutting someone out of our life completely, often with no discussion or warning. There have been many, many warnings along the way to get to this point. But when we are done, we will not make a big deal about being done. We are just going to leave. This includes blocking phone numbers, unfollowing and blocking on all social media and email, and even moving to a different place, depending on the situation.

We can apply a door slam to anyone in an INFJ's life, not just a significant other. We will use it to cut any toxic people out of our lives. INFJs will give everything to our people, but when we are hurt over and repeatedly, there comes a point when we decide that we cannot take any more hurt from this person and it has to stop.

It may seem like it's extreme to outsiders, but INFJs are very sensitive individuals. We put our all into our relationships and are deeply affected by how we're treated, especially by those that we value the most. There is only so much hurt that we can take before we collapse underneath it all.

A door-slam is a solution of self preservation. It's not a first line of defense, though, from the outside, it may seem this way. It's actually a last line of defense. We don't want to use a door-slam, especially on people we love. We don't want conflict and disharmony in our lives at all. It's just that sometimes, we don't have a choice. It's the only option left.

It's not something that we take lightly either. There is a lot of thought and consideration that goes into such measures. A healthy INFJ will realize that there is nothing else that we can do but to cut the toxic person out of our life for good.

INFJs in relationships

INFJs are quiet and peaceful in their lives, and they strive for the same thing in their relationships. We find the best mate and make them feel comfortable and understood in our presence. We give them everything we think they need and expect relatively little in return. If you are lucky enough to have an INFJ in your life, you'll have a companion for a lifetime!

11

Purpose

INFJs are born with a desire to do something big and meaningful with our lives. We often refer to this as our life's purpose. We want to make a big impact on the world. We want to change something for the better and help as many people as we can. It almost feels like it calls us to do this, like our intuition has something built-in telling us we can't stop searching until we find it.

We often struggle with finding it because we don't even know where to start. Our perfectionism and our desire to help people overwhelm us, and we feel helpless to find the solution.

"There are so many limiting beliefs," Kristen Mangus echoed my thoughts when I interviewed her on my podcast.[13] "For almost 2 decades I really had a lot of stress and anxiety around 'What's my purpose?' And unfortunately, I read the book The Purpose-Driven Life in high school. And that really (lead me to believe) I must have a singular purpose that I need to find! I'm here to do this one thing and if I don't find it and figure it out, I'm a total failure!"

I struggled for years with that same mentality. I was convinced there was this one thing that I was born to do that would check all the boxes. This one thing, one job had to:

- Be my hope
- Be my dream
- Give me meaning
- Make my life worth living
- Be a way that I can help people
- Be something I want to do every day
- Pay for my expensive habits and way of living
- Pay for my student loans
- Give me status in the world
- Be the whole reason I was born

That's a lot to ask out of one job, isn't it? I never thought about it when I was going through it, but it really is! We would never make a list like this to ask out of one person. So why do we put everything in our lives into one job? It's just so unrealistic.

Once I let go of all of those expectations, I finally figured out what I wanted to do. It's that simple. Let go before you get what you want. When I finally did that, I found that thing I am supposed to do, and it changed everything. It's like finding true love. People tell you about it and you think maybe they are lying or something because you just can't even imagine feeling that way. That was me for about 32 years of my life. But when I finally found it, I knew it was real.

If you're still searching for your purpose, I want to reassure you it is out there and you will find it. Part of the process is being lost. Every INFJ that I've spoken to about it says that they were lost. So know that you're not alone. You're actually in good company. It's part of the process and you're not doing anything wrong. It's a difficult challenge where struggling is part of how it works. So let's talk about some practical steps to finding your purpose. What does that look like, and where do you start?

Let go

The first step is oh so difficult. It's letting go of expectations. These expectations come from so many places. They usually start with our parents. Our parents want what's best for us, but sometimes they take it too far. Sometimes they try to plan out our lives for us, telling us what they think we should do and pushing us to do that.

Then other people pile on too, grandparents, coaches, teachers, friends. Then you. You have your own list of things you think should be too. But the key to finding your purpose is stepping back from all of those expectations. Let it go.

Let go of:

- What you think your life should be
- What you think you should do
- What everyone else wants you to do

Your life will not be what you think it should be. But that's OK. It can still be something wonderful and amazing. You're struggling to find your purpose because it loses you in something you don't want to do or you don't even know where to start. Either way, I'm sure you have a feeling of what you should do, this thing that's reasonable and responsible and makes enough money to pay off your student loans. But do you really want to be an accountant? Is it your dream in life to be a dental hygienist?

If it is, that's cool! I'm not judging accountants or dental hygienists. But if that's not how you want to spend your life, then why are you in school studying accounting? Why have you spent 10 or 20 years working on a job you hate? Once you let go of the expectations and the feeling that you have to do what you think is responsible, you'll be free to explore what you really want to do.

Explore

The next thing I wronged in my search for purpose was to define it way too narrowly. I thought it was a job that had to be perfect and meet all of my needs for meaning and money. I looked at traditional careers that made sense and were reasonable for a girl in college. The things that mattered to me were status, accomplishment, money, and maintaining my standard of living after school.

If I could go back and do it over again, I would do everything differently. I would explore a lot more things. I would spend a lot of time learning about myself. I would study my personality more, learn about the way to decide and communicate with others. I would think about my values, morals, and what drives me on the inside.

I would also think about what I want my life to look like outside of work. Where in the world do I want to live, what kind of house do I want, what kind of car would I like to drive, what do I do with my free time? I would look at what makes me happy and how I want to spend all of my days.

Then I would explore some things I didn't think would make me happy just to try them out and see. Getting to know yourself, what you like, what you want, what you need... this is the most important step to finding your purpose. How can you know what your purpose is if you don't even know who you are and what you want out of life?

Dream

The next step is to dream. This one is amazing for me because I love to dream. I love to think about what could be. I bet you do too. So I want you to stop for a minute and think about what you really want to do. If you could do anything in the world, what would it be? Is there something at the back of your mind that you want to do that keeps coming up and you keep shoving it down, telling yourself that you can't do it? Pay attention to that. It's important.

I wanted to be a writer for a long time. I loved to read, and I loved that feeling of getting lost in a good book. I wanted to write something amazing that touched people that way. But every time I thought about writing, the doubt would creep in.

You're not a writer. You're terrible at spelling and English. People would laugh if you tried to write something. It would be terrible!

I talked myself out of it every time.

It took years for me to realize that I didn't have to be a good writer to write. I could start by being a bad writer. That was OK. As long as I wanted to write, and I enjoyed it, I would get better. I finally let go of all the expectations and need for perfection and just started writing. And, let's be honest, the early stuff is kinda cringeworthy. But it gets better every time I write something. Now I've written a whole book and more than a year's worth of blog posts!

Whatever you want to do, do it. There is a way for you to make it a career and find your purpose where you're doing something that you love and making money. It is possible.

Finding is the wrong word

We talk about "finding" our purpose like it's lost. We treat it like it's some grand adventure to find lost treasure and like Indiana Jones we need to go looking in the deepest darkest caves of Africa to get it back. This is where we go wrong with our purpose, though. It's not lost. You don't have to find it. In fact, you probably already know what it is.

If you don't know what it is, that's OK. You can create it. Yep, you can create the purpose you want to have. Once you let go of everyone else's expectations of what it should be and you let go of your expectations of what it should be also, you're free to do whatever you want to do. You take some time getting to know yourself, really diving deep into what makes you tick and what you want. And then you connect with others and help them while doing what you want to do. This is the perfect recipe for a life full of purpose and fulfillment. That's all you need!

My experience

I have discovered that the real purpose in my life, the place that I find the most meaning and satisfaction, is helping people through my writing. I knew that I wanted to write when I was young, but I always got caught up in the mindset that I'm not a writer so I couldn't do it. Then I let go of that, and everything changed. I set down my expectations and just write. Do it scared and messy and imperfect. And it changed everything!

I took my writing and a whole list of other things I love, like social media and graphic design, and created a business designed around helping people. I created a community for INFJs to feel seen and heard and understood. I have created this place where people can learn about themselves and feel accepted for who they are. It's truly an amazing feeling! I want people, especially INFJs, to know that we are not broken, we were made the way we are for a reason. Just because we are different doesn't mean that anything is wrong with us. And that it's perfectly fine for us to be exactly who we are.

This is my purpose. This is my life's calling. Everything has changed for me since I figured this out. My whole life is different. My attitude about and dedication to my work is different. It's no longer something that's draining and worrisome. It's fun, and it energizes me. Connecting with other INFJs and helping them go through the same things that I did gives me great joy!

I want to challenge you to do the same thing. Set aside your expectations and think about what you really want. What would make you happy if you could do it every single day? I know that you will find your purpose in life. And if you can't find it, I hope that you will keep looking until you do. I promise you it's out there, even if it's something different from what you think it will be.

12

Career

INFJs look for meaning and depth in all we do. Most of us tie our career to our purpose. I know I did. I grew up thinking there was a perfect career out there for me. I just had to find it. It terrified me to graduate from high school because I did not understand what I wanted to do with my life.

I was so lost trying to pick a major in college that my mom made me take a career counseling course. It taught me all about a bunch of different careers, but it didn't help me one bit. They told me about the job, but they didn't tell me about the people who did those jobs the best. That's really the information that I needed. I know that if I would have known I was an INFJ back then, this process would have been a lot easier.

Most common careers for INFJs

- Counselor
- Clinical psychologist

- Social worker
- Sociologist
- Teacher
- Writer
- Artist
- Graphic designer
- Health Care/Social Service
- Business owner/manager

The most typical careers for INFJs have a few things in common: they help people, they work alone or with only a few people at a time, and they provide a meaningful service to the world. While I strongly agree that, as an INFJ, you can do anything that you set your mind to, I also believe that you will be happier in the long run if you find a job that incorporates a few things that matter most to INFJs.

INFJs Need to Have Meaning In Their Work

It's important to INFJs to work that is meaningful. Connecting with people and being able to help them will bring the most meaning. This makes jobs like counselors, psychologists, doctors, life coaches and spiritual guides very attractive options for us.

Creativity Is Important

I am a super creative person. I love seeing something in my head and then bringing it to life. I also love being able to do things that others can't, like dream, visualize and create. This is how I became a graphic designer. It was something that I picked up in my spare time, and every company that I have worked for has needed one.

Creativity is important in a variety of ways though, not just art and design. INFJs are excellent at seeing the big picture and being able to solve problems that most people cannot. Using insights like this is very helpful in a lot of jobs.

Independence and Flexibility

INFJs find it hard to survive in most corporate jobs. While we are good at following rules that make sense, we struggle to follow rules that make little sense. There are rules in every job that have to be followed, whether or not you like and agree with them. That part can be difficult to swallow.

It's also difficult to follow leaders we do not believe in. This has been the most challenging aspect of working a corporate job for me. I have very high standards for most people in my life, but especially those in positions of authority. I have yet to find a boss I have not lost all respect for at some point, and there is no going back after that happens.

I do not work well with people who micromanage me either. I need some freedom and independence to work on my own. I enjoy working with teams, but I really enjoy doing my thing most of the time.

Variety

I hate doing the same thing repeatedly. It leaves me feeling like my job and life have no meaning, like I am wasting my talents. I need some variety in my days. I need to use my clever insights and creative ideas to change something or fix something.

I have always worked for small companies where I have done a variety of jobs. I was never just a graphic designer. I was the graphic designer/marketing manager/event planner/executive assistant. But I loved learning all of those different things and having a hand in so many areas of the business. I learned so much!

Work environment

Another thing that's important to consider is the environment of the company that you work for. Do you want to work 8 hours a day in a cubicle? Are you OK with working outside all the time? Do you want to be breathing fumes from something in a factory?

When I went into marketing, I did not understand that most marketing agencies have an open office floor plan. I thought nothing could be worse than a cubicle until I interviewed with a company that had tables in the middle of a large room and everyone got a computer and a chair. There was music playing loud and people were talking over each other. It was like a nightmare to my senses. I can't imagine trying to work in that situation every day.

When you're considering what career is right for you, it's important to think about what work environment you're most comfortable with and most productive in. This doesn't mean that all marketing offices are open floor plans, but you have to be aware of it and make sure you ask questions about it early in the interview process.

Think outside of the box

I can't tell you how many times I have read that INFJs enjoy owning their own business. For years, that was not the case for me. I didn't want the headache of all the responsibility. I just wanted to go to work and collect a paycheck. Let someone else make all the rules and decisions. The problem was that I was always unhappy with every job I had. I didn't want to go to work or deal with customers or my bosses. I just wanted to be left alone, to do my work in peace.

But then, I finally found something that I am passionate about, something that I am excited about every time I think about it! Now, I have my business, and I love every minute. The freedom that comes with owning your own business is like that feeling when you first move out of your parents' house or when you graduate from high school. It's scary, but exhilarating at the same time.

INFJs are quiet and calm, people who aren't usually thought of as entrepreneurs. While we can lead, most of the time we'd rather leave that responsibility to someone else. But there are multiple reasons that INFJs make exceptional entrepreneurs. It well suits our personality and demeanor well to do our own thing.

There is nothing like the freedom you feel when you get your first car. You can go anywhere all by yourself. No one looking over your shoulder and watching your every move. There's an even bigger freedom when you move out of your parent's house. It's all up to you, every decision you make is only yours.

That's the same feeling when you start your own business. You have the freedom to do whatever you want. You can run the business how you want to, in the way that makes sense to you, rather than having to abide by someone else's rules. It's an amazing feeling knowing that you can do whatever you want to do.

I've worked in a few jobs where the workspace was just awful. It consisted of old, hand-me-down furniture from decades ago, dirty cubicles, loud coworkers roaming the walkways, people yelling on their speaker phones and slamming doors for no reason.

Over the last few years, we've seen the rise of the open office. It's a whole different hell for an introvert who likes to work in quiet concentration. That just doesn't exist anymore.

One of the perks of owning your own business is that you get to decide what your office looks like. You get to decide what kind of desk you want and what coworkers you want. There's no more adjusting to your environment. You can adjust the environment to fit what you like and need.

INFJs are amazing at long term planning. We have this amazing ability to see things from the logical perspective and from the emotional perspective. Plus, we are killer at thinking things through and seeing what will happen if we go down a certain path. We can see patterns and can predict what will happen based on those patterns. This gives us an amazing ability for long-term planning in our business.

INFJs are also amazing at organizing things in the most efficient and logical manner possible. We consider not only ourselves, but everyone around us in these decisions. We want things to function well for anyone who has to use them.

When you work for yourself, you can set things up exactly how you like them. You don't have to abide by anyone else's rules or standards. You don't have to convince anyone else that you are right and that your way is better. You can establish things that way that you want them.

Most jobs have no real purpose to them. You go to work and do your assigned tasks every day, but does it really make a difference to anyone? Are you changing anyone's life? Are you providing meaning and purpose where there was none before?

It's important for INFJs to produce work that is meaningful. We want to help others in whatever way that we can. We want to do something meaningful with our lives. When you own your own business, what you do is really up to you. And if you find that your work is not meaningful, you have the freedom and the opportunity to shift that work into something is in line with what you want.

Being an entrepreneur is perfect for INFJs

When I was younger, I never saw myself as an entrepreneur. I never wanted the responsibility of making my sales and making all the decisions. I saw working for someone else as being much more stable and reliable. But the older I get, the more I realize that's not true at all. Working for someone else, it's always stable and reliable. It's possible to get laid off or fired. It's possible for those things to happen through no fault of your own.

Laura Charelle, owner of Balanced Bombshells, told me when I interviewed her for my podcast that being an entrepreneur has improved her health dramatically.[14]

"In starting my business... my health improved so much because I didn't have to be around people if I didn't want to be. It really helped create some separation where you can hang out with people and see them when you want and then do your own thing and dive into your creative work."

Being an entrepreneur is perfect for INFJs for a lot of reasons, but mostly because you get to be in control. You don't have to work with people who suck the life out of you. You don't have to go to a place that you hate every day. You can use your creativity and your desire to help others and make money by doing those things!

The most important thing

Whatever career you choose, make sure you are happy doing that work. You'll spend so much of your life in your job, and it's just not worth it to do something you hate. Keep searching until you find that one thing that really lights you up!

13

You're Not Alone

As INFJs, we get stuck in the idea or thought we are alone, because there are so few of us and because we rarely meet someone who understands us. I want you to know that you are not alone in this world, no matter how strongly you feel that emotion. There are at least 77 million other INFJs out there, struggling with the same things you are.

At the beginning of this book, I told you a story about my journey to self-love. It's been fulfilling learning about myself, why I do things and why I think the way I do. Most of it has been an unlearning process, a shedding of all the ideas and beliefs that I've adopted from everyone else.

This understanding of myself has changed my life in so many ways. I'm far more gentle with myself and show myself a lot more grace in difficult times. I know that there are times when I just need time to be, and that's OK. That's part of who I am. That understanding is the beginning of a long journey to self-love.

I hope the contents of this book give you that same understanding and set you on the path forward that you're looking for.

Acknowledgments

There are so many people to thank and so many experiences that have led me down this wonderful and amazing journey.

First of all, I want to thank my teacher from the Introduction to Engineering class who made me take the Myers Briggs assessment for the first time. I don't even remember his name, but he had such a substantial impact on my life. I'm sure he had no idea how it would turn out, but I'm so thankful for that assignment!

I want to thank Cathy Heller, a wonderful and amazing woman who doesn't even know me, but she inspired me all the same, through your amazing podcast, Don't Keep Your Day Job. She made me believe in myself and see the potential in my dreams of writing this book. She inspired me to start my podcast which has given me the opportunity to connect with so many wonderful and amazing people. I've made so many friends through those connections and I'll be forever grateful to her for that!

Thank you to my parents for inspiring me to be the person I am today and for supporting me in sharing my thoughts and feelings with the world. Your love and support mean so much to me and I'm so thankful to have you as parents.

Thank you to my niece Carley for asking so many questions about both of our personality types that I was pushed to learn and be able to explain what I was learning. You've given me a better understanding of myself and those around me and have helped me to be able to teach others as well. You've also encouraged me to see myself as I really am, not how I think I should be or would like to be. Thank you for calling me out when I'm wrong and forcing me to dig deeper and think about things from a new point of view. I love you so much and am so glad to have you as a part of my life!

Thank you to Nikki Gillis for being my first podcast guest and being my wonderful and amazing editor that has pushed me to make this book better than I ever imagined it could be. You are a thoughtful and kind person and I sincerely cherish our friendship!

Thank you to all of the incredible guests I've had on my podcast for sharing your stories and the insights you've gained from your journey. You have made me realize that not only am I not alone in the world as an INFJ, but there are people out there just like me who share the same experiences and emotions. You inspire me to continue to learn and grow and become the best version of myself. Thank you for doing this amazing work and for sharing it with the world. I am truly a better person for knowing you!

What inspires me

A collection of my favorite books, blogs, and podcasts that help me learn about myself and my business.

Books

"Don't Keep Your Day Job" by Cathy Heller
"May Cause Miracles" by Gabrielle Bernstein
"Outliers" by Malcolm Gladwell
"The 5 Second Rule" by Mel Robbins
"The Alter Ego Effect" by Todd Herman
"The Big Leap" by Gay Hendricks
"The Human Magnet Syndrome" by Ross Rosenberg
"Quiet" by Susan Cain

Websites/Blogs

16 Personalities: 16personalities.com
Introvert, Dear: introvertdear.com
Momastery by Glennon Melton: momastery.com/blog
Personality Junkie: personalityjunkie.com
The Myers Briggs Foundation: myersbriggs.org

Podcasts

"Don't Keep Your Day Job" by Cathy Heller
"Do It Scared" by Ruth Soukup
"Revisionist History" by Malcolm Gladwell

End Notes

1. https://www.16personalities.com/infj-personality

2. https://www.census.gov/newsroom/stories/2019/world-popu-lation-day.html

3. https://thequietonespodcast.com/2020/01/11/2-how-to-spread-kindness-as-an-infj-sierra-mafield/

4. https://thequietonespodcast.com/2020/02/18/7-living-a-bal-anced-bombshell-life-how-to-balance-your-hormones-laura-charelle/

5. https://www.dictionary.com/browse/introvert?s=t

6. https://www.dictionary.com/browse/intuition

7. https://www.psychologytoday.com/us/blog/the-intui-tive-compass/201108/what-is-intuition-and-how-do-we-use-it

8. https://imotions.com/blog/difference-feelings-emotions/

9. Numbers from MBTI Manual published by CPP

10. Numbers from MBTI Manual published by CPP

11. https://www. personalityhacker.com

12. http://thequietonespodcast.com/2020/02/18/4-intimacy-as-an-infj-lauren-white/

13. http://thequietonespodcast.com/2020/03/30/episode40/

14. http://thequietonespodcast.com/2020/02/18/7-living-a-balanced-bombshell-life-how-to-balance-your-hormones-laura-charelle/

About Sarah Kuhn

Sarah Kuhn is the writer behind the INFJ Woman brand and the host of The Quiet Ones podcast. Every week Sarah encourages thousands of INFJs to find more purpose in their lives and live their most authentic lives as the rarest MBTI personality type.

Sarah grew up in the Midwestern part of the United States, but moved to the South to finish her education at the University of North Carolina. Her love of learning drove her well past the typical 4 year college degree. She spent 10 years in college, studying Business, Marketing, Criminal Justice and Mechanical Engineering.

After college Sarah pursued her dream of working with professional athletes. She spent 3 years working as a marketing and public relations manager for an agency that managed NASCAR race car drivers along with other professional athletes. Outside of that position she has used her knowledge of business and marketing working in digital marketing in a variety of industries including technology, nonprofit, entertainment and hospitality.

While in college she learned about the MBTI personality assessment which started another research and learning journey for her. Sarah's infatuation with studying personality types grew for more than 8 years and eventually turned into an obsession when she discovered her type was INFJ. She used her knowledge of personality types and her desire to help other INFJs when she started her blog in

2019 called INFJ Woman. To date her blog has over 300,000 views and a following on social media of over 60,000.

In August 2019, she launched her podcast about INFJs called The Quiet Ones. It currently has over 40 episodes out and 40,000 downloads. She's interviewed influential INFJs like psychotherapist Ross Rosenberg, who has done ground breaking research on the effects of narcissism and self-love deficiency.

When she's not writing or recording her podcast, you can find Sarah at home in Boston, exploring the beaches along the Atlantic coast, or spending time with her friends.

Sarah set out with one goal in writing her blog: to help even just one INFJ feel seen and heard and understood. She is dedicated to this path of acceptance, healing and growth in being healthy INFJ women.

INFJ Woman

My story is just like yours. I grew up feeling out of place and had no knowledge of even considering what a personality type was. What's even worse is, I too was plugged into the wrong sources that cost me years of subconsciously believing the worst about myself. Some of those things I believed was that I was weird, different, damaged, broken, unworthy, etc. I later learned that this wrong information was coming from sources/people like family, legal guardians, teachers, bosses or co-workers. Many of you would agree, as an INFJ, our favorite word is "research" because once we start, we can't stop! This is usually the beginning to a path of acceptance, healing and growth.

INFJ Woman is a blog, written from my perspective as an INFJ, about all of the things that matter most to us. My goal in this blog is to create a safe space for other INFJ women to come together, feel you belong and share your stories, while communicating, learning and healing with other INFJ women.

There is an amazing power in hearing someone else's story and realizing it is so much like your own. It gives you that feeling of belonging and helps you to realize that you're not alone in this world!

infjwoman.com

INFJ
Community

Founded by an INFJ, Sarah Kuhn, on a mission to make sure every INFJ feels like they are not alone in this world. This community was created with the goal to make sure every INFJ has a deep understanding of who they are and to make connections with others who are just like us!

Here's what people are saying about it:

"This community is very 'embracing.' Like a warm hug after a long journey away from home."

"It feels like you knocked and the door opens. You're surrounded by people who say "me too" or "I understand". While hearing this, you feel all the tension and hardness from the world melt away. You breathe a sigh of relief, walk through the door, and watch it shut on the rest of the world for the time being."

"I am beginning to see glimmers of hope that I am capable of engaging with people the way I want to - not just the way I "should". This feeling of somehow being connected and maybe even understood without being judged has been a breath of fresh air. Thank you for facilitating more openness and a safe environment."

Come and join this community, that's exclusive to INFJs. We are excited to get to know you and learn about you. In fact, we've been waiting for you!

infjcommunity.com

My story is just like yours. I grew up feeling out of place and had no knowledge of even considering what a personality type was. What's even worse is, I too was plugged into the wrong sources that cost me years of subconsciously believing the worst about myself. Many of you would agree, as an INFJ, our favorite word is "research" because once we start, we can't stop! This is usually the beginning to a path of acceptance, healing and growth.

INFJ Woman is a blog, written from my perspective as an INFJ, about all of the things that matter most to us. My goal in this blog is to create a safe space for other INFJ women to come together, feel you belong and share your stories, while communicating, learning and healing with other INFJ women.

In August 2019, I launched my podcast about INFJs called The Quiet Ones. It currently has over 40 episodes out and 40,000 downloads. I've interviewed influential INFJs like psychotherapist Ross Rosenberg, who has done ground breaking research on the effects of narcissism and self-love deficiency.

There is an amazing power in hearing someone else's story and realizing it is so much like your own. It gives you that feeling of belonging and helps you to realize that you're not alone in this world!

The Quiet Ones is available on all major podcast platforms.

thequietonespodcast.com

CPSIA information can be obtained
at www.ICGtesting.com
Printed in the USA
LVHW011522110723
752163LV00004B/162